www.kristysinsara.org
©2017 Kristy Sinsara
#ninjalife

Cover Creative Director: Julia Junkin

Cover Graphic Designer: Melissa Tugmon

Content Editing: Ashtyn Ryan, Julia Junkin, Kris Prochaska,
Cylvia Hayes, Jennifer Morey, Jane Hiatt & Sheryl Mobley

Cover Pictures: Carol Sternkopf Photography

Inside Jacket Picture: Four Daughters Photography

Editing Notes: Blue Fish Circle Publishing

ISBN-13:978-1981743056
ISBN-10:1981743057

ACKNOWLEDGEMENTS & DEDICATION

To all of my Facebook friends, and all who support me on social media: You have truly made this journey possible for me, and my heart is sincerely overwhelmed with gratitude for you. This book is dedicated to all of you.

Special thanks to Ashtyn, Kris, Julia and Jane for helping me discover my own truths within myself that allowed the space for this book. I feel like you all had ringside seats to the epic change that took place in my life, as you all took turns in the ring, helping me find myself.

Thank you to Laurie & Kara Hudson for being the first human beings to ever say the words to me, "Responsibility is the key to freedom" ... apparently you were correct! You were the first two people in my life who truly saw my ability to stand up, and be present in this world.

To Ashtyn Ryan, The Love of My Life: Thank you for allowing me the space to be me, in this world, and always epically supporting all that I do. (And for enduring 7 solid hours of guitar playing of the same song while I try to channel some strange creative energy).

Shout out to the Oxford Hotel in Bend, Oregon and its amazing staff: Thank you for letting me hole up for a solid week while finishing this project. You guys are amazing. Your staff is amazing. Your hotel is gorgeous!

And lastly, to **MY FUTURE SELF**, the woman on the mountain in my dreams: Thank you for reminding me that you exist. Thank you for always being present. Thank you for continuing to make me accountable each and every day.

#WWMFSD

A NOTE FROM THE AUTHOR

If you're anything like me you're about to skip right over this part and go straight to Chapter One - Part One. Don't do that. Trust me. This part will set you up for **HOW** you need to read this, and **WHAT** you are about to read. Don't get all *"ADD"* on me, and skip over this important part and assume you know best as to where to begin reading. **THIS** is where you should begin...

I sat down to write a book about *"how to get your life back on track after you've epically f*cked it up"* (which was the original title). However, what I ended up writing was more of a personal memoir of unbelievable tales - from triumphs to tribulations, of self-destructive behavior, to the ultimate self-awareness.

From homelessness to attempting several suicides, to constantly creating enemies, to being my own worst enemy, to breaking my life down to a level that was unrecognizable... To finally finding freedom within and success of epic proportions professionally. **YES**, I have finally discovered the way to peace after a life of total chaos.

I used to think I needed to avoid all of the train wrecks in life. Until one day, I realized that I had become the train wreck. I had become the picture below the *"warning"* sign. I had taken all of the abuse I had suffered as a kid and I had somehow become the abuser, just in different ways. And, I had spent a life justifying every shitty decision and every fucked-up moment. Because, I had given myself a free pass to self-destruction... As if to say, *"If they can abuse me... well, so can I."*

I took my father's mental illness and I became mentally ill, on different levels. I took the despondency of my mother and became distant from the world around me to a point of imploding.

I was obsessed with feeling abandoned from the world around me. I was literally possessed with this idea that the people only wanted to use me. I could not ever just feel good enough.

If the wind blew wrong, it was just one more reason why I should just kill myself, end the madness and stop the "*crazy*" that had become my life. I was always on the verge of "*destruction*" because I was always standing in the middle of chaos. Even if the world around me seemed peaceful, everything still felt like anarchy and confusion. The chaos never subsided within me.

I COULD NOT SETTLE. I could never fully breathe. And, I certainly couldn't allow myself to ever become immobile... for it is in the quiet space of reality where the silence becomes an overwhelming force of truth. You realize in those moments that you are lost. You have no single idea how to find your way back home.

I searched for truth anywhere I could look and I wandered this fucking world over looking for something that would set right with my soul... bring me back "*home.*"

Therapy, church, people, sex, alcohol, careers, money... it all came back empty for me. It all made me feel more empty inside. Until one day, I realized that this was the problem. I had to stop looking for myself outside of myself. But, that's not easy to tell someone who has been self-loathing for over 40 years... "*to turn within...*" and "*tell the truth?*" These are two epically, fucking difficult things to hear when you have been doing everything possible to NOT look at yourself... to avoid truth at all costs. However, it was the excruciating first step... taking full responsibility for who I had become, where my life was and ultimately coming to terms with the fact that I had personally participated in living my life (or purposefully not participated).

If you've ever felt lost, (to the point that you question if "lost" is just where you live) – If you've ever felt broken, (to the point where you've questioned whether "*broken*" is just who you are) - If you've ever felt pointless, (to the level of wondering if you should even carry on in life) - If you've ever felt ashamed, (to the point where you have lied so much about your life you can't even remember what was truth from fiction) - And, if you've ever gotten to a point where you're standing on the edge and you just can't do "*this*" anymore... You are truly willing to give up, or give in to change... **THIS IS YOUR BOOK.**

I wrote the fucking screenplay on self-destruction. But I also wrote it on self-healing, and learning to grow forward. Say this prayer, and open your mind: "*I acknowledge that there are no accidents in the Universe. And I know that I am here, reading these words for a reason. I am ready for change. I am ready to discover new truths, and I am ready to heal, to forgive, to accept responsibility, and to become the person I was sent here to become.*"

NAMASTÉ, MY FRIEND. WELCOME TO YOUR FUTURE!

"*I've come to believe that there exists in the universe something I call "The Physics of The Quest" – a force of nature governed by laws as real as the laws of gravity or momentum. And the rule of Quest Physics maybe goes like this: "If you are brave enough to leave behind everything familiar and comforting (which can be anything from your house to your bitter old resentments) and set out on a truth-seeking journey (either externally or internally), and if you are truly willing to regard everything that happens to you on that journey as a clue, and if you accept everyone you meet along the way as a teacher, and if you are prepared – most of all – to face (and forgive) some very difficult realities about yourself... then truth will not be withheld from you.*" – Elizabeth Gilbert, Eat, Pray, Love

WHY TAKE RESPONSIBILITY?

When I was talking to a friend recently about writing this book, the very first thing she asked me is, "Why would anyone want to take epic responsibility? What's in it for them? What's on the other side of that obviously difficult life journey?"

Well, that's a great question! I won't sugar coat this for you. Taking a heroic level of responsibility takes more than a modicum of strength, a surrendering of the will, and a complete yielding of the ego, that very few people are truly capable of facilitating.

Simply stated, it is not easy to choose to take responsibility for things in our lives, especially not for those things that have deeply hurt us or left us broken and bleeding on the surface of our existence.

We live in a world where we accept (or deflect) blame and then we neatly place it in a space that feels "comfortable" and acceptable emotionally, rather than reflecting on truth. Why? Simply because the alternative is more difficult to accept. We will always choose first that which comes easiest and feels best.

But the reality still remains that if you can truly discover the strength within you to stand in the epicenter of your own life and allow your spirit to grow from a place that is responsible for all that it has encountered; here, in this space, you will discover a new awareness that births an elevated consciousness like you have never known before.

WAKE UP!

"I beseech you therefore brethren, by the mercy of God... And be not conformed to this world: but be ye transformed by the renewing of your mind." - Romans 12:1-2 King James Version (KJV)

The time has come for you to understand the simple reality that this book will reflect: **YOU ARE IN CONTROL OF YOUR LIFE, AND YOU ARE RESPONSIBLE FOR ALL THAT YOU HAVE EXPERIENCED.**

You are about to climb a mountain before you, and just as when you physically climb a mountain, you will have moments of clarity, moments of chaos, moments of stress and fear, and potentially moments of total confusion. However, at the top of this mountain lies a power, harnessed by self-awareness, that will enable your soul to venture beyond any place you have ever known before.

Responsibility is the key to your freedom.

I urge you to take this great challenge with me; and proclaim that from this moment forward you accept the full responsibility for all of it...are you ready?

THE STORY OF THE CHICKEN MAN:

There once was a man who lived in Philadelphia who everyone referred to as "Chicken Man." He would walk around the city with a feather in his hair. He had a toy chicken adorned to the top of his car, and he would drive around town making chicken noises. When he got out of his car, he had two little baby carriages with two little dolls and a picture of a woman. If you ever said something to him or came near him, you could hear him making the sounds of a chicken.

Everyone used to laugh at Chicken Man assuming he was just crazy, until one day someone learned about his story.

See, Chicken Man woke up one morning around 3am and his house was on fire. He instantly panicked and leapt out of the window next to him... only to get outside and hear his wife and his two children screaming for help. He attempted to run back inside to save them, only to realize the flames had become too powerful and the fire was too overwhelming for him to be able to get back in. He tried with all of his might to get back in, and he couldn't. He could hear them crying for him, screaming for help and there was nothing he could do to save them. Eventually the cries stopped, and his entire family perished in the fire.

A little while later, his brother-in-law came over and realized his sister and kids had died in the fire. When he discovered that his sister and the kids had died but Chicken Man had survived, he instantly started beating him over and over, saying, "You chicken! How could you let your family die? You're nothing but a fucking chicken, you let your family die. You're nothing but a coward. How could you, you fucking chicken..." beating him over and over with his fists... and with these words.

When a fireman pulled him off Chicken Man, he said, "Hey, are you alright?" The Chicken Man started squawking like a chicken... and from that moment forward, in his life, he only made the noises of a chicken.

For years, everyone in the city of Philadelphia thought this man was just crazy. They discarded him as another city nuisance, a mentally unstable nut job.

The truth however, is that he was only crazy with grief. The reality of his one single, spontaneous decision was too tremendous to bear.

Chicken Man is a great example of why most people do not want to accept full responsibility – because they can't see past the act of responsibility. Most people believe that if you take responsibility then you'll be forced to spend a life in turmoil and grief, as Chicken Man did.

However, that's not true. Yes, he is a perfect example of what happens if this is where you leave responsibility. It will eat at your soul, debilitate your spirit, and eventually consume your life. But you must accept it, and then become equally committed to healing from it, and forgiving yourself through it.

The point of accepting responsibility is not to beat the shit out of yourself emotionally or to feel defeated. It's to do the opposite. It's the ultimate act of self-love.

However, taking honest responsibility is a four-part quest, which we will delve into in later sections.

Part one: accepting it fully. Part two: healing from it and learning to forgive yourself. Part three: changing because of it and growing through it. Part four: giving back in life through your new perspective of wholeness.

Once you've accepted and forgiven, you must discover the purpose of it all; **for there is a purpose in your pain.** You called forth the lesson, not the action. Stay committed to the why, not the what.

At the core of this book lies the truth within me, that responsibility is the key to my freedom, because the absence of it is the single thing that has hurt me the most in this life, by myself, and from others.

Therefore I proclaim FREEDOM. And I admit that I am wholly in control and responsible for all that I experience from this moment forward.

"It's never what broke you open that matters...
It's what it broke open that you should focus on."

PERSONAL LIFE INVENTORY

We are going to start by taking a journey through your life...

Take a deep breath (literally, right now, take a deep breath), and promise yourself one single, solid thing... that you'll be willing to be honest with yourself in a way that you never have been before this moment.

There's no reason to continue to lie to yourself. No one can hear your thoughts. So stop being afraid of the whole truth within you; because ultimately it will be your willingness to be truly honest with yourself that will begin your journey to freedom.

This isn't a book you read out loud, snuggled up next to your partner as you lay beside a winter fire, sipping Pinot in your chiffon night robes. This is a book you read with a highlighter in hand, a notebook beside you, and perhaps have a box of tissue readily available. We're going to go deep here people... so get ready.

You are here because you are fucking sick of living the life you've been living. You're reading this now because you're ready to stop the madness and end the bullshit in your life. You're tired of the *"same scenario – different person,"* constantly chasing and never catching, constantly running and getting nowhere (but exhausted) in life.

There is only one desire within you, that must be present in order for your life to change... Your desire to change must be stronger than the comfortable security of the bullshit you're living in. Your need for something more must surpass your desire to stay *"as is."*

You must be willing to be honest, take action and move forward.

YOU HAVE TO LEARN SOME KEY RULES IN THE BEGINNING:

Everything is your fault. (don't get pissed at this, just keep reading)...

There are no mistakes in the Universe.
You are wholly in control of your life!
This is **YOUR** journey, no one else's.
No more blaming.

I don't care if you were abused, or your parents lavished more love on you than a Sultan Queen – there's a reason why you're feeling broken and lost... and that reason may or may not have anything to do with your parents.

I believe that we chose this life before we got here. I believe that we knew that it would be the experiences we had that were necessary for our spirits to grow.

I love the line in Troy where Achilles' says, "*It is the gods who envy us. For a moment in time we get to be human and feel all of the capacity of human life.*" It is a pleasure to feel pain, for it is the pain that reminds us of the pleasure. It is a great fortune to stand in darkness, for the darkest of days truly illuminates the brightest lights ahead. And, as Achilles pointed out, it is a great honor to get to be human for a moment, where we exist in the realm of growth and possibilities.

THE ULTIMATE CONFLICT - REFLECTIONS AND CONTRAST

The truth is that we learn everything in life through contrast and reflection. We can't possibly see life otherwise because we become conditioned to accept what we've always known.

Have you ever considered the fact that you have never actually seen yourself in any capacity except by a reflection? It's not even possible for you to see yourself without a reflection, you'd have to disconnect your eyes from your head and turn them around, and at that point they wouldn't work. The only way you can see yourself is by seeing yourself through the reflection or lens of something other than yourself (i.e. a mirror, a camera, a picture, etc).

In the same way, most of us have never learned the joy of any single experience other than through contrast.

I grew up fantasizing about what it would be like to have a daddy who just wanted to love me, hold me and play with me. I wanted to have the kind of father that I saw in the movies; one who protected me, a mentor to look up to, a hand to hold when I was scared, not one who wanted to physically abuse me and sexually assault me. How wonderful would a life be with a father I could actually call "*Daddy?*"

But if I had the choice today, between being who I have become or a much lesser version of myself, I'm going to choose the shitty fucking childhood experiences (with that shitty dad I never asked for).

Because in the end, whenever I see old friends from my childhood and I realize "*holy shit... they really did peak in high school,*" I feel grateful that I didn't have that experience.

I used to envy the shit out of one of my friends in junior high, whose mom I thought was so freaking cool. She would allow us to drink, she'd sit in the hot tub and laugh with us... and talk to us about sex and boys, and how she used to do drugs in the 60's. We'd talk about all kinds of things we shouldn't actually have been talking about at the age of 12. She literally taught me how to smoke a cigarette.

I envied my friend and her relationship with her mom so much it drove me nuts.

Then, I ran into this friend when I was 25 years old and asked her how her mom was. She said, "*I don't know. We don't talk anymore. She became a raging alcoholic, basically turned into a selfish lunatic and left us.*"

I remember telling her about how jealous I used to be of her relationship with her mom, to which she said, "*Are you kidding me? All I ever wanted my whole life, was to have a real mom... one that cared about what time I went to bed, not tried to keep me up talking to her while she drank a bottle of Vodka. I used to be so jealous of all of my friends, who had parents who made rules in their homes. Everyone was jealous of me because I got to do what I wanted, but all I ever really wanted was for someone to love me enough to tell me what to do.*"

And then these epic words fell from her lips... "*It's all good though. Having that kind of mom taught me to be a better mom. My daughter and I have an incredible relationship because of what I never had growing up.*"

And there you have it folks... the truth of contrast.

PEOPLE ARE RARELY WHO WE WANT... BUT THEY ARE ALWAYS WHO WE NEED. People are rarely who we want... but they are always who we need. People are rarely who we want them to be but they are always who we need them to be!

She needed her mom to teach her how to be a great mom, in the same way that I needed my mom to teach me... through contrast.

Now don't be a douche canoe, and try to find something wrong with the foundational basis for this argument of contrast and lessons. I'm not saying that *"if you had amazing, loving, affectionate parents, you'll never learn to be one yourself."* I'm saying that most people, like me especially, learn things by experiencing the opposite of it.

It's a powerful understanding of who you are and the reality of your life... one that can truly help you move forward in a much healthier way. At some point, you need to take a look at your life and realize that you may be one of these people. And if you are, then you can take a fucking breath for once in your life and realize that **YOU NEEDED ALL THAT YOU EXPERIENCED.** It was no accident that you didn't get what you wanted. You got what you needed!

The whole Universe was conspiring **FOR YOU** when it didn't give you those amazing parents who threw you a *"coming out party,"* when you finally admitted you were gay.

The Universe was conspiring for you when you weren't that cute as a child and realized that you needed to focus on and strengthen other attributes more than your looks. And now, you're a sex kitten **AND** you've got a killer personality. BOOM!

The Universe was conspiring for you when you accidentally walked into a New Years Eve party at the wrong house and ended up spending 8 hours partying at the House of The Nigerian Embassy, with statesmen and debutants from all over the world.

Okay, maybe these are all just my personal experiences, but you have your own.

Spend a moment right now and just think about the things that were "*accidental*" or seemed "*wrong*" at the time, yet ended up being epic blessings in the end.

The Universe has always been conspiring for you.

Everyone has always been what you needed, regardless of whether you wanted it. And there has never been a moment where anything went wrong. It is as it was supposed to be for you.

And much like my favorite Mark Twain quote: "*The two most important days of a man's life are the day he was born and the day he discovers why.*" The two most important days of your life are the day you realize that ALL of life bends to your will and nothing has ever been an accident. The Universe has always been conspiring for you.

IT'S TIME TO MOVE ON...

One of my favorite lines from Anna and the King is the line where Anna says to the King's son, "*Most people see the world as they are, and not as it actually is.*" I have never heard a truer statement about life and conditioning.

Conditioning kills our perspective. This is why moving a lot or changing the scenery in our lives is epically vital to our outlook in life.

I remember the first time I had ever visited the city of San Francisco. My friends and I had driven over the Golden Gate Bridge, and we sat on the bay in Marin County, overlooking the city, and I remember feeling awed by the beauty around me.

And as I was taking in this magnificent, epic moment, breathing in a new experience, my friend said, "*I'm so sick of looking out at a bunch of buildings and lights. I wish I could just see trees and open fields.*"

We become so conditioned to what we have experienced over and over that we forget to see the beauty all around us.

Because I had spent my life growing up in a small town in Oklahoma, I had come to appreciate the beauty of a big city skyline; so a moment in my life seeing the lights reflecting off of the San Francisco Bay seemed magical.

However, my friend said there was nothing as beautiful as seeing an open field of trees, unscathed by humanity. In this moment, my friend and I were actually experiencing the same thing. We were seeing the same thing, it's just that our experiences were being filtered through our own lives. We were both, however, appreciating contrast yet filtering through our conditioning.

If it were not for my father, I would never know how important it is to take the time to talk to children when you're upset with them, and not react emotionally; to teach them things, not take your anger out on them. If it were not for my mother, I would not know the importance of holding a child in your arms and showing them affection. If it were not for the things I never received, I would not be as grateful for the things I did. The lessons taught to me by my parents, albeit difficult to grow through, all created this mega giant of a human being that I am today.

You may not feel like a mega giant, quite yet, but I promise you that if you're willing to do the work, you will. You will find this space that I have found, where it all makes sense in the end. Where gratitude for it all overwhelms your heart.

Yes, I grew up abused, feeling discarded and unloved. However, it is the reality that the independence these experiences created within me is what allowed me to have the epic levels of success that I have had in life.

I started my first business when I was 25 years old with $400, and a year later a man flew to Oklahoma from New York City and offered to buy it for $135,000.00.

I have owned several successful businesses. I've done things that others believed was impossible. I have stretched the boundaries, and raised the roof, and have spent my life constantly proving that there are no limitations on anything, ever.

I do not believe for a second that I would be half of the greatness that I have become if it were not for the abuse suffered as a child.

WHAT HAVE YOU TAKEN RESPONSIBILITY FOR?

Let's take some inventory here. What have you actually taken responsibility for, and what have you placed onto someone else?

A friend of mine told me how disappointed she was that her ex-husband left her and their children and moved to Arizona to start a new life (after an affair that he had). She has spent the greater part of the last decade judging and blaming him for his decision to do this.

Every time she tells the story there is always blame and never a moment of responsibility on her part. So one day I asked her what it was that caused him to have an affair. Was he just one of those annoyingly insecure men who needed to seek attention from women instead of working on himself?

And she said, "*No. He had an affair because he was upset with me because I had cheated on him with his best friend a few months before that.*"

Wait. What the hell? "*I've heard you tell the story about what a piece of shit your asshole ex-husband is for years and years; how immature he was for leaving you, what a horrible father he is for leaving the kids. All I've ever heard is how he is bad, and you are innocent. And you've known all along why he cheated, and yet never thought it was an important part of the equation to help you grow through this experience?*"

And she said, "*Ya, well, I cheated...but I never left.*"

Well...that's a gross mis-characterization of truth, to say the words, "*I cheated but I never left.*" For one, cheating **IS** leaving. If you've cheated, you've left a part of the relationship already.

But in this moment I finally recognized why, after ten years, she has not been able to move past this pain, to grow and heal; because she's not being honest with herself about what happened and her own culpability in this.

The outlying layer of this story, the one that's easy to see, is that he is a bad dad for leaving his children. And it's not until you pierce the veil of this cover that you realize the truth beyond the excuses, and the pretty package of blame she has created.

I'm not going to honey coat this for you, sugar tits. The minute you chose to have an affair, you left your children, too. Let's call a spade a spade. You're just as freaking selfish and culpable in this scenario. And if you'd stop blaming him and be willing to open your heart to the reality that this was a two-way street to destruction that you both participated in, you'll begin to heal.

And I'll venture a bet that says, once you begin to heal, you'll probably also be able to begin cultivating a very healthy relationship with him, and pave a way for your children to do the same.

Your entire family healing is dependent upon everyone taking responsibility for their own culpability in whatever scenario broke you down.

Responsibility is key in healing. It is mandatory. This one single action will determine a great deal of your future.

I also think it's important to understand why she doesn't want to take any responsibility, or hasn't yet.

The truth is that if she were to take responsibility in this scenario, then she must also admit that (in part) because of her action, her children no longer have a relationship with their father. And that truth is a daunting reality to accept, for most.

This woman grew up without a father. Her dad left her at an early age as well, and she swore up and down that she would never put her children in the same situation that her mother put her in... but she did.

And why... is a whole other issue to explore.

(PART 1-ISH)

RELATIONSHIPS 101

THE ULTIMATE PLAY OF YOUR LIFE - YOU ARE THE AUTHOR AND THIS LIFE IS YOUR PLAY

I believe one of the best ways to take back control over your life is to realize that your life is truly like a play, being played out as your life. The truth is that you have the power to change any scene, any scenario, any character, any ending, at any point that you want. **YOU ARE** the writer, and the director.

And just like a writer/director, you have all of the power to yell, "CUT! *This isn't working for me! Let me change this up and add different characters, change the backdrop, and rewrite the ending.*" **YES**, you possess this level of power. This is your life, this play is being written by you, and you alone.

However, the crazy part to remember is that this play and the outcomes to the scenarios in each scene are not being written with your words; they are being written with your beliefs. What has manifested before you, in the screenplay of your life, are the beliefs within you. Those beliefs created the scenarios and characters around you.

It's important for you to realize that your life is not a sum of your hopes and dreams and desires. It's a sum of your beliefs. It's a totality of all that you think you know that you know that you know.

So let's talk about this play, and let's start with the characters involved, and let's talk about what you think you know.

THE CHARACTERS OF YOUR PLAY

The truth is that every single person in our lives is a mirror image of ourselves. We have called them all forth to illuminate something within ourselves. We have manifested every person and every issue that person brings to our table.

When your life feels like it's on auto repeat, and you keep dealing with the same shit through different people, it's because there's a lesson in that situation that you haven't gotten yet, something that you're not seeing – as you were meant to see it. The scene ended without resolution, and therefore must be replayed. And it will continue to replay until the purpose is discovered in that moment.

Most people get stuck on the characters and forget that the characters are merely there to play out a scene. It wasn't about that random man who used and abused you... it's about the reality that you let him. And he will continue to show up as different people playing the same character until you understand why.

Most people will say that you are the "main" character of this masterful play, but what I'm here to tell you is that you are actually ALL of the characters. You are the mother and the child. You are the abused and the abuser. You are the giver and the taker. You are abounded and abased, in different scenarios. Just hear me out...

I sat with a friend last night at dinner that admitted she had been having an affair with a married man. She was bawling giant elephant tears telling me how disgusted she felt... especially because just a few years prior to that moment her own husband of 12 years had left her for another woman he had been having an affair with.

"How could I have done this? I know better than to be with someone who is married!"

My response... well let's be honest here... for one, when you were going through this, you repeatedly said (at least a hundred million times), *"How could anyone do this? How could a woman sleep with another woman's husband?"*

Well, sweet cheeks... now you know. And now, here you are... once the cheated on... now the cheater.

You asked a question, and the Universe provided the answer. In your face. No denying it. Crystal clear. **NOW** you know. And for the first time since your divorce you not only understand *"how"* a woman could have sex with a married man, you also understand the deeper issue... of *"why?"*

It's important to remember that our judgments of other people have far more to say about us then they do about the people we are judging. And, as many religious scriptures all agree, what goes around comes around, full circle.

However, I think it's imperative that you understand that it doesn't come back around full circle to punish you, but rather, it comes back around full circle to TEACH you. So learn what needed to be learned, and move forward with more grace, forgiveness, and understanding.

I believe it is imperative that, even in the moments where we are the innocent ones in any given situation, our innocence is not an invitation to judge. It is an invitation to exude grace, understanding, and forgiveness.

I am fascinated with the truth of tis friend that she stated for years, over and over, "*HOW COULD SOMEONE DO THIS?*" And she was given the answer by being faced with the same situation. And in that moment, she chose the exact same thing. And now she is feeling more shame than ever before.

BELIEVE ME WHEN I SAY: YOU WILL BECOME ALL THAT YOU JUDGE IN THIS WORLD.

THE RECURRING ROLES

So in the middle of our lives, if we are living mindfully (and honestly), we begin to realize that many of the characters in the play of our lives seem to be recurring roles, played by different actors. And we notice that we, too, are continuing to play the same roles over and over.

This is why you feel like you're in the same situation, different person... Same character, different actor... Same scene, Same thoughts... Same mistakes, Same shit... Different day.

As I was contemplating this chapter, I started really considering the specific recurring roles that keep coming back, scene after scene, in my own life.

If you'll consider this honestly, you'll start to realize that you've manifested the same scenario in different forms.

Perhaps your dad was despondent or abusive, and one day, ten years into your marriage, you've realized you've "married" him. Your mom never gave you the affection you so-desperately longed for, and you suddenly realize your wife is exactly the same. Your bosses all have the same underlying theme of "not seeing your true talent," or perhaps you always seem to have the same problem with all of your friends.

THE PARADOX OF MY PERSONALITY

I realized a few short years ago that almost 100% of the issues people have with me arise from a single truth: I am not an effective and honest communicator - if I think there is any tension on the table, or potential for any unpleasant feelings towards me. As much as I truly do not care about other people's opinion of me (and I really do not), I am still a people pleaser for those I am in personal relationships with, and it pains me beyond measure to let someone down.

However, it is my refusal to ever address this issue that ultimately leads to letting everyone down.

I can stand on a stage and proclaim a personal opinion that I know would offend the masses, and think nothing of it. However, if we are in a personal relationship, chances are I'll have a really hard time telling you that I'm too busy to meet next Tuesday because I have too many deadlines I should be prioritizing otherwise.

Had I just called and said, *"I'm sorry, I really can't do this project right now"*, I would avoid so much strife in the end. But I fear that saying that may cause you to not like me anymore, so I overstretch my schedule, and I over-promise my ability to finish something on time, and I say what I think needs to be said in order for you to not be mad at me.

... and then I cancel.

I'd rather cancel over the phone, then let you down in person.

People assumed that someone as outspoken as me would have no problem saying what I needed to say, and this is true in front of a crowd of 10,000, however one-on-one... that's scary shit to me.

This scenario played out over... and over... and over... a thousand times over in my lifetime, until I was finally willing to (a) admit it was an issue and (b) figure out what was the underlying core issue within me? Why was I exhibiting this behavior?

This scene played out so much that I became known for not showing up for appointments? I became the ultimate queen of cancellations.

You know how I realized this? Not through deep reflection and meditation. But because I suddenly started realizing that every single person who made an appointment with me would double and triple check whether or not I was going to truly show up.

And when I was questioned, I would laugh, flippantly shrugging it off as nonsense... as if... I would never show up... come on.

If there is a consistency in the behavior around us, we must look at the behavior within us.

What I had realized is that I am a flake. I was not acting as the reliable person I saw myself as. And it actually hurt me to admit that, (it hurt me to type it) but it's a true statement.

So in order to fix this behavior, I had to turn within and figure out what in the hell I was doing this for. Why was I canceling so many appointments that people were afraid to even make them to begin with? Why was I afraid to not schedule something? What in the hell is going on with me?

This is where I realized, as much of a paradox as it may be, that I am a people pleaser at the core of me. Not for the masses, which serves my ability to write books and entertain with blatant honesty with my blogs and posts... but for my personal relationships.

So where does this fear stem from?

I had to truly reflect on this issue... and I realized an epic self-discovery... that I have mad, crazy, insane abandonment issues... and if I fear that if there's any chance someone will be upset with me, it will lead to them deserting me. So I do damage control by pleasing them... although it always actually ends in them "*not*" pleased with me.

At the core of me, I am actually a very reliable person. It's actually wildly important to me that people trust that I'll do what I say I'm going to do, and I'll be where I commit to being.

But what I had discovered is that my abandonment issues superseded my desire to have a good reputation, and/or my need to be a reputable person. This behavior was causing me to cultivate a bad reputation, and an even worse self-worth conflict than I already had.

43-year-old Kristy, the business woman, believes it's paramount to have honor with your word... however the little girl in me, who still feels fear that people will desert her as they all did when she was only 3, was making most of these decisions. And 43-year-old Kristy gets a shitty reputation for it in the end.

(We are going to discuss all of this in later chapters)...

So how did I fix it?

First, admitting that I am guilty of this behavior.

Next, being willing to discover why, at the core, and do the honest, self-reflective work needed to work through this shit.

And finally, do everything in my power to ensure that my actions speak louder than my words.

Also, I acknowledged this pattern, and apologized to those most affected.

If I say I will be there now, you bet your ass **I WILL BE THERE**. And I otherwise, offer blatant, hard core truth to all inquires for my time.

Have you ever seen that t-shirt that says, *"I'm sorry I'm late but I didn't want to come."* I love that t-shirt. It accurately describes half of the reasons people now get angry with me.

But it feels better to be hated for who I am, than loved for who I am not. In the same way that it feels better to have someone upset with me for being honest, rather than upset with me due to my incapability of facing the truth.

"No. I can't make that appointment at 10:00am because I usually work until like 3 or 4am, and meeting with anyone (especially you) before noon sounds like some form of Chinese torture. How about 4pm, and I'll bring the coffee?"

And... suddenly no one is angry.

Unlike public school in America... all lessons are repeated until learned. **YOU WILL NOT GRADUATE TO THE NEXT CLASS** until you learn what you are suppose to learn.

So the question is **WHAT SCENES** do you keep showing up over and over again? What rolls? Who is playing them? And how are they ever different from the others like them?

Again, our recurring roles are played by other actors in our lives, but the scene remains the same; and it will continue to show up continuously until you're willing to be honest about what it is about this scene that you're not getting. So one of the easy ways to break this down is to consider **ALL** of the characters of the screenplay of your life.

THE CHARACTERS OF MY LIFE PLAY

[THE NARCISSIST-CHARACTER]

People get the definition of a narcissist wrong. They will say things like, "*He is always talking about himself, what a narcissist.*"

However, this character cannot be relegated to a simple lack of social skills. The highlight of this character is that they are shockingly non-empathetic towards you. Trust me, if you have a narcissist in front of you, you have some serious, deep-seeded self-worth issues you need to be working on love muffin! Their inability to "*concern themselves with your petty issues*" is the least of your problems.

They're not in your life to do anything but highlight what is already within you... Your deep-seeded lack of self-worth/respect. **Someone can't make you feel anything, ever. People only highlight how you already feel inside. This is just one of the more crass forms of a mirror we manifest in our lives.**

If this character makes you feel used and discarded, they're only highlighting what you're already doing to yourself, and how you're already feeling.

You're going to try to play the "*victim*" role here, but you'll soon discover, if you're truly self-reflecting, that they are only treating you equally as bad as you have been treating yourself.

True Narcissists are incapable of seeing that they're Narcissists. It's actually a mental disorder (according to a therapist friend of mine), and they aren't going to be changed by your incapability of "*dealing with them.*"

Narcissists are nothing more than mirrors for the purpose of self-healing. Do not try to make this relationship anymore than it is. Trust me, don't waste your time.

I have a very good friend of mine who recently got out of marriage with a Narcissist. One of my favorite stories she's shared (to highlight his behavior) is this: She had spent her entire marriage to him catering to his every need. Dinner every night on the table when he got home. House always cleaned. Kid always taken care of, despite the fact that she worked too, it was her responsibility (according to him) to care for him, the kids, and the house.

He had grown up with one of those mothers who also catered to his every need and over-praised his every action. She raised him to believe that the Universe centered around him, and she wanted him to find a woman who took over this role in her life. And... she did!

One day my friend called her husband and said she "*just can't do dinner that night for them.*" She had a hard day, and needed a reprieve, to which he replied, "*Not a problem. Don't worry, I've got it handled.*"

She was shocked. She was pleasantly surprised to hear him not get upset, and ecstatic to know that he was being so compassionate and loving, and take care of her for once.

Later that evening he came home from work with a to-go bag from a local restaurant in hand. She was so excited to see what he's brought home... and so hungry. But then he immediately sat down on the couch, opened up the bag, laid all of the food out that he had bought (for one), and began eating.

She asked, "*Where is our food?*" (referring to her and their son), to which he responded, "*Why would I get you food? I don't know what you want to eat. I told you I would take care of dinner. This means I'll take care of me. Why would I get you dinner?*"

And if you had asked him about this situation, he would have astonishingly responded with the reality that he does not see what's wrong with this scenario.

This is classic Narcissist behavior. Not only are they unconcerned for your needs, but they can't even see that being unconcerned is something wrong.

BUT it's important to note that their presence in your life is not to make you a victim, but to highlight the reality that THEY are only mirroring your self-abuse within you. They don't lack respect for you any more than you actually lack respect for yourself. As crass as a narcissist may be the truth is that they don't hold any more weight of apathy for you than you do.

This character will continue to reappear over and over until you realize that it is the fear, doubt, insecurity and lacking of self-love within you that is manifesting their presence before you.

My friend didn't leave her husband after this incident or many others that followed. She stayed, she played the victim, she kept thinking that catering to him (more) would eventually cause him to give back (even just a little). Yet, it never did... and it never will... because they never can.

You can't give something that you don't have to give. It's a simple theory to understand.

This character in my life never shows up as a lover or a co-worker. Somehow they have only shown up as a kid or a parent. However, it doesn't matter what form this character takes. It is still your responsibility to delve into the deeper issue of why they are continuing to pay out in different scenes over and over.

When I questioned my friend about why she stayed in this marriage for so long her response was, "*I was hoping that he would change.*"

Listen people. My wild spirited, apathetic Siberian Husky is more likely to change behavior and suddenly start caring for my feelings than your human is. She's more likely to write me an apology letter for sprinting off out of control every single time I try and let her out to pee, than your partner is.

> Narcissists are not in your life
> so you can change **THEM.**
>
> They're in your life
> so that you can change **YOU.**

Word to the wise while dealing with one of these characters:

Don't chase their affection. Don't allow them to be in a place of power of you. Do not allow them to believe they have the upper hand. Do not hide your feelings to save their temper. Do not dismiss your own needs to cater to their every whim. And do not act like a victim every single time they dismiss you, and treat you like shit. **GET OUT OF THE RELATIONSHIP,** and do yourself a favor and seek counseling to discover why you were there to begin with!

You can't help someone who doesn't realize they need to be helped. And by definition alone of a Narcissist, they are unaware that anything is wrong with them. And all of your greatness, or kindness, or love, or lack of self-respect, or mutual self abuse won't fix them!

[THE "ABUSED KID" (AKA "THE VICTIM") - CHARACTER]

"*It's not my fault.*" This is the only line this character ever really needs to know, because it's essentially all they ever say. Literally. To freaking everything.

However, much like Jane Hiatt described in the foreword, this character doesn't always mean "*it's not my fault*" as much as they mean to say, "*I didn't mean to do it.*"

It's important to realize there is a significant difference between these two statements. One states, "*I have no culpability, and refuse all forms of responsibility,*" while the other states, "*I am embarrassed, and just don't know where to go from here.*"

I know the deeper truths of this character because it is the role I've played most often; and if I'm not playing it, it's standing in front of me being played out by someone really close to me.

It's the role where there is never any honest self-reflection in any situation. And there's enough "*drama*" in the relationship that I can point a finger to anything close by and prove that nothing chaotic around me is because of me.

I wrote the play-book for this character, and so I become exhaustively irritated when anyone tries to use my own plays against me.

I literally never used to take any responsibility for anything. If a bill didn't get paid, it was because someone forgot to give it to me. If my car ran out of gas, it's because I was too busy helping someone else to even notice I needed gas. If I hurt someone's feelings, it's because they provoked me to the point of being shitty... and the apology that follows

(if there is one) is flippant, and insincere, and motivated only by a need to "*move past any discussion of personal responsibility.*"

Nothing is ever the fault of the victim... and most of them have some degree of "*abuse*" in their life that becomes illuminated and used as an "*excuse*" the minute responsibility is mandated.

(It's not my fault I'm having fun).

I got a job once working for a great firm in Southern California, and I decided (as all incredibly responsible 20-something-year-old's do) that I should call in sick on my first day of work and go to Six Flags Magic Mountain with all of my friends instead.

Unfortunately, however, I accidentally forgot to call in before leaving the house, so once we arrived at the amusement park I immediately searched for the nearest pay phone (this, of course, was before the world of cell phones).

And so, as I'm calling my new boss to explain to her that I am just too sick to come into work (and I'm really playing it up here people), right as I begin to "*fake cough,*" and "*fake sneeze*", suddenly a roller coaster goes over my head with the screaming sounds of joy echoing through the phone and all around me.

And my heart sank.
And I realized I'd been caught.
And I knew I'd fucked up.
And I was thinking "*what a dipshit I am.*"

And I was wracking my brain, trying to think of something, and I came up with...."*My ride to work this morning took me to an amusement park. I had no idea where we were going. I was so tired, I fell asleep on the ride here; and when I woke up, we were here. And I want to come in I just don't have any way back.*"

And... I never heard from them again.

But you see what I did there? My natural proclivity was to skirt responsibility. My natural response was to say, "*It wasn't my fault.*"

And as ridiculous as this story is, it's indicative of my conditioning to believe that "*truth*" equals punishment, not reward. I'm not saying that being honest with my boss in that moment would have gotten her to allow me to keep my job, but I am illustrating how quickly we take this position whenever we are faced with any immediate blatant need to take responsibility.

But here's the healing part... Once I was willing to be honest about the fact that I was always skirting responsibility and never being honest with myself, I was finally genuinely able to understand why! Why is an important part of the equation here.

I had discovered, through my honest, responsible self-reflection that the reason I had a constant propensity to "*skirt responsibility*" was in part because I had grown up being severely beaten for things that were truly not my fault.

I grew up in a home where I was getting the living shit beaten out of me for things I legitimately didn't do; so I sure as hell wasn't about to admit to anything that I actually did do.

And this behavior (over time) leads to a habit from the conditioning of my mind: "**TRUTH EQUALS SEVERE PUNISHMENT,**" this is what my childhood taught me; therefore, I should always protect myself and never be honest.

However, as Jane said before, how we often translate the words, "*I didn't do it,*" isn't always a word-for-word truth, as much as the deeper underlying interpretation of "*I simply didn't mean to do it.*" And, it's important that we are mindful of this behavior and learn to change accordingly.

I was able to change my behavior patterns by being honest with myself and understanding why. What I mean, specifically, is that I wasn't always meaning to lie, or evade truth, as much as I was meaning to avoid ridicule, and evade unnecessary pain.

I have never actually had a desire to lie to anyone, I have, however, had a survival instinct to protect myself, at all costs. Understanding this truth was paramount for my self-awareness process, and ability to accept responsibility.

[THE UNREQUITED LOVE - CHARACTER]

This is the "*constant reminder that you're not worthy or good enough for anything*" character in your life.

The irony of this character for me is that you would think that "*if I didn't feel good enough*" about myself I certainly wouldn't be chasing after someone I felt was "*better than me.*" But this is exactly what you do when you don't' feel good enough. You call forth the truth within you to stand in front of you, as a mirror reflection of that truth.

Remember, we always manifest before us that which we believe, not that which we want to believe.

We always manifest someone who illuminates the truth, not the desire. I manifest people who remind me that I'm insecure, not someone who manifests that I wish I didn't feel this way.

I have spent my life never feeling good enough... and so I spent my life feeding that machine within me.

I chased jobs and romantic partners and situations that I felt "*not good enough for*" (usually subconsciously) just so I could use these people and situations to prove me wrong (or right, for that matter). But situations and people can't change how we feel about ourselves.

Sure, a hot chick who can't stop making out with you can certainly make you feel attractive, if and when you otherwise don't; but it won't last. This doesn't change the core of you; it only changes the moment.

The truth is that **EVERYTHING I HAVE CHASED, I HAVE ALSO CAUGHT.** And none of it has ever fulfilled me.

LEGALLY TRUE

When I was 27, I applied for a job as a college professor at a 2-year college in OKC. I was the only person applying who didn't have (at least) a Masters Degree.

When I submitted my resume, the lady chuckled at me as one would a two-year old who is trying to sneak by you to get to a cookie jar. She said, *"Honey, this position is only for those with advanced degrees. I'm sorry."*

Instead of saying *"Okay, that makes sense"* and walking away in that moment, I decided to research who did the hiring for professors, and how.

I discovered that it was a *"board of directors"* who convened for each interview, and ultimately who hired the candidates. So I drove to the school the next day and went into the office of the man who was the head of the board, and I told him that not allowing me an interview could be one of the greatest mistakes he's ever made. I explained to him that he doesn't know me, but I know me. And I know that I could be a better professor than anyone he's ever worked with. I'm not asking him to hire me; I'm asking for a single chance at a single interview.

A week later I received a call that they're wiling to schedule an interview, an action motivated by this man's curiosity. I went into the interview in my newly-purchased suit from *"The Limited"* I had just bought the night before at the local mall.

And I went in like a fucking force to be reckoned with. In this moment, I am dominant. I am sure of myself. I am knowledgeable on the subject matter for which I desired to teach. I am indomitable in my abilities to bring a new level of awareness and excitement to the school. I am a fucking super hero.

The next day I received another call back for another interview. And another interview...

And five interviews later... out of all other candidates, all of whom had teaching experience and their Doctorate Degrees, I **WAS HIRED** as the youngest professor ever to teach at City College. (Boom. Drop Mic).

But... you know what happened after I started teaching? Although I found it to be epically fulfilling in many ways, I was bored of it, because the reason I wanted the job was nothing more than to prove to myself that I was good enough to have it.

I taught myself that getting things I felt like I shouldn't be getting was a sign that I was worthy of more.

I have spent my life chasing romantic partners, careers, money, positions, status, affection, love, and people... and I've eventually caught it all... ONLY to discover the same thing I did when I was 27 years old standing in front of my classroom at City College... That I **wasn't there because it reflected who I was or wanted to be, but because of what I wanted to prove.**

And no relationship that is birthed from a need to prove something will ever be sustainable.

[THE "I'LL NEVER PLEASE THEM" - CHARACTER]

Unlike the Unrequited Lover - Character, this person is usually in some position of authority over me. And this is the character who, no matter what I ever do, I can never quite please. I'm constantly seeking their validation, and they are constantly telling me to fuck off, or more likely than not, not even acknowledging my existence enough to even bother telling me to fuck off. But I'm addicted to their inability to make me feel worthy.

The only difference between this character and the romantic character is that this one only holds authority over me. There is no other form of relationship involved. I am addicted to pleasing them.

When I was in my mid-20's I began working for a brilliant lawyer in Oklahoma City who had made a name for himself by settling personal injury cases that were otherwise not accepted by other attorneys.

He was brilliant.
He was dynamic and charismatic.
He was handsome.
And he was wildly successful.

And there was nothing I could ever do to get a "*great job*" out of him. I spent years and years trying to do this creative thing and that creative thing, trying to pull an "*atta girl*" out of him. Nope. Nothing. Ever.

I once wrote a Writ of Certiorari that was so brilliantly cultivated, and later successful, that it was referred to in a subsequent meeting of the Oklahoma Bar Association. And when I brought this up to my boss, he responded by saying, "*Oh, really?*"

I spent years working as a paralegal for this man, and then one day he randomly walked into my office and said, "*You should really just go to law school some day. You're too smart to just be a paralegal.*" That was his way of calling me brilliant.

And when he said it, it was like the heavens opened up and angels floated down, singing the "*Hallelujah*" chorus.

I got what I wanted, in that moment. And you know what? Not so coincidentally, after getting his compliment, and after six years of working for him, I soon after this moment quit.

Why did I quit... because it was no longer a challenge to me?

Or did I quit because he no longer mirrored my desire to believe that I wasn't "*worthy.*" The minute he gave me what I had been chasing I felt an intense lack of need to please him.

The point being that I thought I was chasing a need for him to make me feel good about myself, however what I was really attracted to was his incapability to acknowledge me, as I had refused to acknowledge myself. He was my great mirror of self-doubt.

I wasn't looking for him to make me feel something I couldn't feel on my own, I was looking for him to substantiate my fears within me, all of my insecurities, and my doubts about my self-worth.

People reinforce our own beliefs about ourselves. No one can give you something you're incapable of giving yourself. It's not possible.

The point of these two characters (the "Unrequited Love" and the "I'll Never Please Them)" is that you will never be satisfied by someone giving you something you are not able to give yourself. Whatever they do offer you will never be enough. It will never seem like enough. Because what you're missing isn't what's not being given to you by someone else, it's what's not being given to you by yourself!

[THE ABUSER (OR USER) - CHARACTER]

This character frustrates the shit out of you. You know in your heart that you should not have a relationship with this person, but every single unhealthy thing about them feels "*normal*" and "*comfortable*" to you.

They are actually only in your life to show you how far you are from self-love, self-respect, and being whole and healed.

You excuse their shitty behavior because you have an insanely high tolerance for being abused and used, and you also have a remarkable ability to "*empathize*" with people's shitty behavior. They are only a mirror of your lack of growth. They are not a relationship that will be sustainable past self-awareness and healing. So worry not, you won't always be dealing with them.

I have both been with this role and played this role. And when I am the one playing it, I am always matched up against someone who has the same self-worth issues I do.

Both people in this relationship are mirroring the same issue in one another.

DADDY WHAT?

A friend of mine told me recently that he only wants to date women with "*daddy issues.*"

"*How can you tell which women have daddy issues?*" I asked.

His response: "*It's easy. The girls with daddy issues never say no because they don't want to disappoint you. You can barely give them a compliment and they fucking swim in it for days. You tell them you don't like something and they bend over backwards to fix it. Women who don't have daddy issues* **NEVER** *try to prove anything. So how can I tell? I throw a little, tiny, shitty line out, like something that challenges their self-worth, and if they are still talking to me afterwards, I* **KNOW.**"

As we begin discussing this desire of his to seek women with "*daddy issues,*" he later reveals that he is actually aware that it only stems from his own internal, deep-seeded insecurity and "*mommy issues*" of his own.

His mom left home when he and his brothers were very young, and ever since then he has been chasing after the affection of women. But he's wildly unsure of who he is as a man and feels responsible for his mom leaving. So (in his own words), "*instead of dealing with the core of what's going on emotionally, I choose to stay distant and just escape into the world of two people never really knowing themselves or each other. It's just easier that way.*"

I think it's important to know that at the other end of abuse is a human being who feels just as bad as you do.

Believe me when I say that whether you're the abused or the abuser in this (adult) relationship, you're mirroring the same thing within each other. There's nothing to judge here. One is just as lost as the other.

So stop being a victim and acting like someone is "*abusing*" you with their distance or mean words, and start taking some responsibility for how you're attracting it.

[THE UNGRATEFUL EMPLOYEE - CHARACTER]

I opened my first business when I was 21 years old, and that is when this character showed up in my play. This character has literally come back to each and every single scene where I am the business owner, and he or she is always the wildly insubordinate employee who refuses to respect what I need from them.

I keep thinking, like a parent giving into their wildly destructive child, that as long as I give them everything they need and want and more, they will love and respect me in the end. But the relationship with this character, in every single scene, ends with drama and chaos. And me... in the end... feeling like a victim (again).

This character feeds straight into my need to be liked, and respected, and loved. And I have this delusional idea that if I give them everything, they'll go to the mountain tops and proclaim my generosity and kindness to the world over.

But you know what happens every single freaking time I have them before me? The relationship ends in utter chaos, with them doing the exact opposite of anything I wanted.

GRAPHICALLY SCREWED

My firm worked with a graphic designer who I literally gave everything to – I allowed him to make his own hours, paid him more than he requested, and I did anything I could think of to make him like me more.

And when I had to let him go, he went to the mountaintops and told everyone how horrible of a human being I was. He even expressed that he actually didn't have any personal experiences with me ever being horrible to him, but that didn't matter because he "*found out things*" about my past and used every single thing he could find to try to use it against me.

He tried to coerce me into paying him "*hush*" money; he went online and blasted me; he called one of the radio stations I was working for and tried to get me fired; he wrote letters to everyone he could think of who had the authority to hurt me. He would not stop.

And when I said to him, "*What on earth did I ever do to you to make you do these things?*" Here was his response: "You think you're better than me and you're not; and I'll never stop trying to destroy you to prove it."

I was dumbfounded. Where did that come from? I mean, he admitted that I had never actually done anything to him personally, so where was this sudden disdain for me coming from?

It came from the mirror between us. I mirrored his deep-seeded lack of self-worth, and he mirrored mine. And even though I was the boss and he was the "*worker*," we were in the same position energetically with this issue between us.

Truthfully, he was probably the most disrespectful human being I have ever worked with in my life; but I never said anything to him about his lack of respect. I never told him how much it bothered me that he never treated me with kindness. I just let him. Then finally one day I put my foot down and said, "*You're not allowed to speak to me like this anymore, and you can't treat me this dismissively and with so little respect.*" And he stood there and told me to "*fuck off*" because "*he could do whatever he wanted to do.*"

In that moment, he was right. I had actually taught him that he could do anything he wanted to do. And the day I finally stood up for myself and said "*I'm not going to allow this behavior any longer,*" he went bat-shit crazy on me.

The Ungrateful Employee character in my life kept showing up over and over (albeit never as bad as this last one I just described) because I was constantly feeling like I never deserved to be the "*boss*" in the situation. I always felt "*less than*" with many of my employees I've had over the years, and the truth of my insecurities within me showed up in my behavior towards many of them.

[THE "I CAN'T DO THIS WITHOUT YOU"
BUSINESS PARTNER - CHARACTER]

This is the person I have manifested in my life who I think is going to mask the dark and deep black hole of self-doubt that always existed within me. This person will come down to the realization that it has nothing to do with what you want to DO with them, but what you want to **PROVE** with them.

Do you know who Motley Crue is....? For those of you who don't know who they are, they are one of the most successful 80's rock hair bands.

They sing many songs I'm quite sure you'd recognize, although I admittedly had to "*Google*" them myself. Oh, yea.... "*Girls, Girls, Girls*" and "*Shout at the Devil*" and many other songs that I remember blasting during my childhood.

A few years ago I wrote a book called, "*How to Build Your Business Using Social Media.*" About a year after it was published, I received a call from a friend stating that Vince Neil, the lead singer of Motley Crue, was looking for a new online social media public relations consultant. An interview was scheduled, and I met with him and his girlfriend, Rain Hannah. He instantly hired me!

I had a sweet place in my heart for working with him because I instantly realized that this man in front of me was the writer of the words that my brother had tattooed over his heart, "*Home Sweet Home.*" You know I'm a dreamer...

I had many amazing experiences working with Vince that I will die remembering fondly and with absolute gratitude.

However, I will be known not for my work with him, but for how our relationship ended.

See, I was so determined that I was not good enough for him, that I actually agreed to work with him without financial compensation, and agreed to only be compensated by him giving me a *"shout out"* on the social media pages I was building for him, letting everyone in the world know that I was *"good enough."*

I mean, I practically contracted those exact freaking words. I said, *"Instead of you paying me every month, how about you just give me a shout out when my next book gets published so that people know that they're worth buying?"*

"Um... okay," he immediately agreed.

I wish I could say, *"I'm not sure what I was thinking,"* but I knew exactly what I was thinking.

I knew exactly how I was feeling, and I knew that I was about to let him take advantage of me because he was a big rock star, and working with him was going to translate to the world that **I AM GOOD ENOUGH**, for once!

But the exact opposite literally came about from this relationship. It was as if the Universe said, *"Cue the epic fucking reality we have in store for Kristy Sinsara."*

Within a few weeks of working for Vince Neil, I had recreated a new social media platform for him on Facebook. Where his previous engagements were roughly 18 people per month, I had taken to hundreds of thousands per month (literally). Yes, I am actually quite good at my job as a social media strategist.

I'll cut to the chase, and make a very (very) long story short.

This epic experience ended with us fighting (well, actually me fighting with his girlfriend), and me getting a phone call one afternoon from the Associated Press, with a woman on the other line asking if I'd like to make a statement about the fact that Vince Neil just sued me for control over his social media platforms.

"What in the hell are you talking about?" I asked.

So, Vince Neil filed a lawsuit against me claiming that I had not allowed him access to his social media pages. After making some phones calls and hiring an attorney, I realized that this lawsuit was not actually anything that Vince understood, as it was actually being led by his girlfriend, Rain Hannah.

And... here's the mirror....

What I had discovered through my relationship with Vince was that his girlfriend, Rain, although a beautiful woman, is a wildly insecure human being. She and I were the same human being in this one single way. We both felt deeply insecure and unworthy of the good things in life. She felt as insecure as I did, just in other ways. And she and I constantly mirrored this issue between us, throughout my entire relationship with Vince.

We both sought control.
We both sought constant recognition.
We both sought to be held in higher positions in our lives than the positions we felt mirrored in our hearts.

She let him treat her like shit, cheat on her, drink too much around her and dismiss her feelings constantly...

Just as I let him work me into the ground constantly, without compensation; feeling tired, used and exhausted by it all in the end. But, I kept trucking through because I was chasing a need to feel "*good enough*" through it all. "*If someone like Vince Neil told the world that I was good... then it meant I was truly "worthy."* Just like Rain thought, "If Vince Neil wants me... then I must be attractive and desirable."

In the end we discovered that it was his personal manager, Dana Strum, who had actually allowed this entire thing to get out of hand because he wasn't strong enough to stand up to anyone around him. He had spent years on his own using Vince as much as he could to promote his own band.

But for me, it all came down to the truth that I gave up something I actually should not have given up just so I could be seen as someone who was worthy.

I gave up my self-respect, and I looked to someone to give me something I was refusing to give myself: "*self-worth.*" The ridiculous reality of this actually makes me laugh a little as I type this. The fact that I was looking to someone outside of me to give me "*self-worth.*"

Many people told me to "*sue him back for the damage that he caused to my reputation;*" but (for one) he didn't cause damage to it, he only highlighted through his lawsuit that I was a badass social media strategist and the world took notice. I also didn't counter-sue because, in my heart, I knew why I had gotten myself in this situation. I knew that there were internal things happening here beyond anything anyone could ever see.

And, I knew that I was culpable in the breaking point of this relationship for the very same reasons I entered into it to begin with. What allowed me to get into it is the ultimate truth that took me out of it: The full circle reality that I had entered into a relationship as a victim, when I was never ever anything of the sort.

WILD, EPIC, SELF-HONESTY leads to incredible heights of self-discovery on levels you can't understand until you do it.

It elevates you above this human realm, where you would never seek to sue one another, because you understand the cosmic truth surrounding each and every single situation. There is a greater truth here within you. A truth that no lawsuit could ever find... or heal.

[THE "FAN" - CHARACTER]

Of course there's always the character who thinks I'm amazing – no matter what I do, I can't do wrong. They're always on the sidelines of my life cheering me on, believing in me, defending my fuck ups, supporting my shit, excusing my ridiculous decisions, and never actually reminding me to take any responsibility for anything, ever.

This character could also be called *"The Enabler."* *"Enablers"* feel like *"Fans,"* and their words and actions sometimes feel like *"love,"* but in the end, they're actually one of the biggest antagonists of our plays. They're the wolf in sheep clothing making us believe that their presence in our life is positive.

They're worse than the ones you call *"Enemies."* Their presence in your life is more insidious than someone who is blatantly abusing you, because almost everything they do, all of their actions and words, feels good to us.

Most people spend their lives surrounded by mostly "Fan" characters. In fact, there are many people who actually refuse to be in a space where there are no *"Fans"* around.

They can't go anywhere unless there is someone present who is feeding into every single one of their deep-seeded insecurities. So, how can you tell whether someone is a *"Fan"* character in your life play? It's simple.

Consider which one of your friends is always excusing your behavior and never bringing to your awareness the consideration that you may ever be wrong. Who never pushes you beyond your level of comfort? Who is always willing to give you the accolades or excuses you're always longing for? This is your wolf in sheep's clothing.

This is who you call when you're fighting with someone, and you know they're going to automatically be on your side. This person is the worst person you can actually have in your life. I know because my entire world used to only be filled with them.

And during this time, my entire world was stagnant, as I was growing increasingly further away from my truth. Because truth and freedom can only be found in responsibility, and responsibility isn't a word a "*Fan*" Character will ever use with you.

Do yourself a favor right now, and make a list of the characters in your play. If I were you, I'd start here. Who are your biggest "*Fans?*"

MAKE A LIST OF ALL THE RECURING ROLES YOU CONTINUE TO CREATE IN YOUR PLAY

THERE ARE MANY, MANY RECURRING ROLES IN MY LIFE:

- The cool client that I really want to like me, so I bend over backwards for them, and jump through hoops, and the relationship ends in complete and utter chaos, simply because the hoop jumping and backwards bending has only caused them to devalue me in some capacity.

- The friend who thinks I'm "*not there enough for them.*"

- The honest friend/therapist who thinks I'm not taking enough responsibility for my actions.

- The distant friend who always thinks I'm "*famous*" and who deep inside truly resents me.

- The "*close friend*" who swears he/she will always be honest with me, who walks around my life constantly pointing out my faults.

The public interest of self-awareness – Creating a small crowd around me of people who wildly adore me, yet never actually really get to know me on any honest level.

THE TRUTH IS that the world is a mirror image of ourselves, and every single one of these characters in my life have something to teach me about myself. I continue to manifest them all, over and over.

There are also many *"non-recurring"* roles, where the character makes a cameo or plays the supporting lead role for a moment, in a specific scene.

However, it matters not, whether they are in the scene for a lifetime or if they are making a quick cameo appearance. They are **ALL** a mirror image of **YOU**.

SO WHY DO THE SAME CHARACTERS KEEP COMING BACK?

It's simple. Because you're not learning the lesson necessary to learn! You're not learning and growing through the situation. And that lack of growth is evidenced by the fact that the same character keeps showing up, and that scene keeps ending in the same way.

Do you know how to determine when you've grown?

When the recurring-role character shows up, and you change the ending of the scene. When the super douche-canoe appears, and you instantly recognize him and the fact that he's clearly incapable of offering you what you need, and you don't chase – in fact you don't even "entertain" him anymore. You look at him and think, *"This isn't for me."* And you walk away. End scene.

And then you know how you know when you've actually learned the lesson in its entirety?

When you stop manifesting this character altogether in your life!

When you have stopped manifesting the scene, you are ready to move forward. LIFE LESSONS, unlike public schools, don't allow you to continue to the next level unless you truly have fully grasped the concept of the lesson at hand.

WE NOW KNOW WHICH CHARACTERS YOU KEEP CREATING AS A MIRROR IMAGE.

BUT IT'S ALSO IMPORTANT TO BE AWARE OF THE RECURRING ROLES YOU CONTINUE TO PLAY.

It's also important to ask yourself why you continue to play these specific roles over and over. What's at the core of this character for you?

At the core of my characters lies a single, common denominator:
I DO NOT FEEL GOOD ENOUGH...

... to **BE** in relationships
... to **DO** things on my own
... to **HAVE** things without help
... to **GO** places I've never known
... to **LIVE** a way I know I should be living
... to **SAY** things I really want to say
... to **ACT** and **REACT** to things authentically

In all scenarios in my world, the reality is that my "*self-worth*" issues always present themselves... have caused me great pain, strife, chaos, confusion and more self-doubt.

So... where did this come from? Why don't I have the ability to just **BE** me because I'm scared that no one truly wants me?

Consider for yourself right now all of the recurring roles you've played and you've seen play out in others consistently throughout your life.

Write them down. And be epically honest about them..... if only to yourself.

_____

_____

_____

_____

_____

_____

_____

After we have mindfully and honestly considered these manifested roles, whether within us or in front of us, it's important to stop and understand why and how they are there.

This means that it's imperative that we do some internal exploring, starting all the way to the beginning of this incredible journey here we call this human existence.

I'm going to walk you through my journey and show you how it became quite obvious why I was manifesting the same roles, placing me in a position of "_proving myself,_" "_hustling for love,_" "_acting out,_" etc.

(PART 2)

THE BREAKDOWN

WHAT THE HELL HAPPENED TO ME?

Many people follow me online, literally from all over the world, to read my daily inspirational messages on Facebook or enjoy one of my unapologetically written blogs on life, or love, or all of the above.

But the truth is that I wasn't always "*this.*" I wasn't always engaging, inspirational, or even fun to be around. This person that I have become literally took me 43 years to find, to create and to accept.

I was once a jaded, angry, resentful human being who refused to participate in meaningful conversation, who repeatedly denied the chances to allow people to "get close to me," and who was so absorbed in my disdain for authority that I would purposely self sabotage anything in front of me that possessed even the slightest elements of power over me.

I grew up hating this life.
I grew up resenting the world around me.
I grew up fucking loathing myself on a level that I would (just for fun) fantasize about how amazing and cool it would be to kill myself... and I'd consider all the ways to do it.

The story of my birth and adoption started out sounding like an adventure of a lifetime, looking much like a "made-for-tv movie" (highlighting the impossible journey of a loving couple and their adopted children). It all quickly turned into a haunted childhood full of darkness, abuse and anger.

I'm going to share with you, some of my most vulnerable, personal experiences simply so I can show you how, in the end, I was able to use the single concept of responsibility to grow through so much pain that I endured.

THE FOUNDATION FOR A BEAUTIFUL LIFE OF BULLSHIT

So my story in this lifetime starts out as a wildly improbable, incredibly inspiring tale of 3 people who seemingly loved me so greatly that the lengths to which they traveled to save me were truly miraculous.

My birth mother was from the province of Ubon Ratchathani, where the Thai, Laos, and Cambodian borders meet. There she lived with her parents, my brother, and myself, in a tiny wooden structured home on stilts above the Mun River. When I was 3 years old, she realized she could no longer afford to keep me; so she traveled to the city of Bangkok and placed me in an orphanage.

About a week later, a young couple from a small town in Oklahoma, who were recently stationed on the island of Guam, had heard about the orphanage. The couple was told that they couldn't have biological children of their own, and had adopted a little boy from Topeka, Kansas, two years prior to being stationed. So the three of them traveled to Bangkok one weekend to the orphanage. The story I have always been told is that they walked in and saw this plump 3-year-old toddler standing on a chair looking out the window, and their adopted son, Scott, immediately yelled, *"There she is, that's my sister."*

So they decided to adopt me.

They were told the paperwork was going to take two weeks to complete, so they had to leave me there. However, when they came back two weeks later I was gone. My birth mother, apparently sick with guilt and sadness, had traveled back to the city of Bangkok to retrieve me.

Here's the miracle part: Most people in that moment would choose another child available. But instead they chose to hire a translator and a tour guide. They took a plane, a train and a boat to the province of Ubon to come find me.

They found the house I was living in, convinced my birth mom to let them take me back to the United States to live with them, and offered her an undisclosed amount of money (of which I've always assumed was clearly in the trillions). She accepted, and voilá! **HERE I AM.**

So... yeah, that story is really cool. I mean it's epically freaking cool, and totally improbable actually.

The most beautiful part of this story is that the little boy, who fought so hard to get me (to find me, to keep me), would turn out to be the closest relationship I have ever experienced in this lifetime. The bond he and I formed was pretty incredible... and that bond began immediately.

When I was adopted I only spoke Thai and my new family only spoke English; so my new parents found communicating with me challenging and frustrating. The interesting part is that somehow my new brother, who was 4 ½ when I was adopted, was able to somehow always perfectly translate what I needed, or what I was trying to communicate, without skipping a beat. We both spoke different languages and yet spent hours communicating.

So Scott and I traveled back to the United States with our new parents, and we settled in (what was then) the tiny town of Moore, Oklahoma. And all was right with the world.

PLOT TWIST

A couple of years later, in an unexpected twist of events, our parents ended up getting pregnant. Nine months later our little sister was born.

Within six months of her birth we were suddenly, and unexpectedly, thrown into this whirlwind of change and confusion. We suddenly became the "*other*" kids, and we couldn't figure out why.

My brother was so young when he was adopted, that he had no memory of it; and by the time I had moved to the United States, I too had forgotten where I had come from. In our minds, we just assumed that our parents were our biological parents. Therefore in our minds, this little baby was just like us.

I mean, as a kid, you don't have some cognitive thought process of where you came from if nothing is ever discussed otherwise, you just assume this is where you came from.

No one ever told Scott and me that we were adopted. So when we see this new little kid in our home is being treated so significantly different, we can't understand why.

We also couldn't understand why she was suddenly being compared to, as if she were more like our parents than us; how much she looks like them, and acts like them; has their hair or eyes or stature, and not us.

I remember my grandma being at our house and saying, "*She has your head shape, Pat.*" And me immediately quipping back, "*Do I have your head shape too mom?*"

They all just laughed....and I didn't get it. I couldn't fathom why it was even funny. Why wouldn't I have my mom's head shape?

I truly felt constantly confused as to why I was always left out of the equation when discussing *"family traits that were passed down."*

They never told us we were adopted. And truthfully, when we were really young it never seemed that obvious. I'm darker skinned but my dad had some Native American in him. So, no one would suspect unless otherwise known. My brother was lighter skinned like my mom, and had bright blonde hair. Certainly no one suspected he was adopted.

We were truly confused by how this kid was any different than us. Until we discovered the truth, that is...

OMG YOU DON'T BELONG HERE

Our parents never took the time to explain anything at all to us. I was 11 years old when I finally discovered the truth, and the only reason we ended up discovering we were adopted was because my brother went snooping through our dad's desk one day and found my adoption paperwork in one of his drawers.

He comes screaming into my room, "**Oh My God, SIS.** *You don't even belong to us. Our parents adopted you. We're not even your real family.*"

So when my parents got home we immediately asked them what this was all about. Was it true? Was I really from a different family? Where did I come from? Who am I? Where are my real parents? Tell me everything!

My parents admitted that I was adopted and told me that I was from Thailand, but otherwise didn't tell me much of anything else. I just assumed they didn't know anything else. They certainly didn't tell the story I shared above.

I didn't find any of that out until later when I was researching my return to Thailand in my early 20's (which, for the record, is a trip I will be taking in 2018 for the first time ever).

I look back now and realize how much more I would have understood life and myself, had they just taken the time to explain anything in any more detail.

TALK TO YOUR ADOPTED KIDS

I think it's important that kids understand their backgrounds, their heritage, and their history. My parents never took the time to even show me where Thailand was located on a map. I remember suddenly realizing it in a junior high geography class, and being incredibly shocked that it was on the other side of the earth.

If you have adopted children, please do everything possible to help them fill in the blanks in their minds. Whether they are capable of expressing it or not, they know something is missing, and the answers you can provide help adopted children put all of the pieces together. And all of the pieces together help children like me become self-aware far sooner in life.

Even though we don't know why, adopted kids "*feel*" the difference, even if there is no disconnect. There is still something in our minds and hearts that knows there is more to be explored here.

Back to the moment our parents are confessing....

The only part I actually remember of the conversation was my brother taunting me the entire conversation, thinking it was hilarious.... until he too learned that he was adopted.

My dad said, "*Well, Scott, hold on a minute. I wouldn't be so quick to make fun of your sister. The truth is that we adopted you too.*"

His eyes swelled up. His face sunk. His reaction was a little different than mine. Since the moment my brother found my adoption paperwork I was like, "*Oh this is epically cool.*" My brother, on the other hand, immediately burst into tears, and his one and only question was, "*Why did my parents give me away?*"

I admittedly thought the adoption was a very cool thing to learn about. The only negative experience I had from being adopted was listening to my mom freely state in front of me (literally my entire life) that *"you never know what you're going to get when you adopt. It's a scary thing to take someone else's kid."* (as if every freaking kid on the planet being raised by their biological parents has a greater chance at being a better person).

Either way, it was indirectly beaten into our hearts: the shame and the constant feeling of lacking worthiness for not being their biological kids.

No adopted child should ever hear his parents say, *"Adopting is a gamble, you just never know."*

DO NOT TREAT YOUR ADOPTED KIDS DIFFERENTLY

And if there is one single thing I would beg of any parents who adopt a child, whether domestic or international, it's this: Please do not ever differentiate your treatment between your adopted children and your biological children. I believe it is truly a form of *"adoption abuse."* And if you don't have the capacity to treat all of your children equally, with an equal proportion of love, time, money, energy, etc., don't bother adopting. You're not doing any kids any favors by adopting them and then abandoning them, emotionally or otherwise.

And for the LOVE OF GOD, please do not ever say (in front of them especially) *"adopting a child is a gamble,"* or any *"shame"* statement. Never shame your adopted kids for not being your biological children.

THE DAY THE WORLD CHANGED

My father grew more and more despondent with my brother and me after my sister was born. He went from reading us bedtime stories to not even speaking to us half of the time; and the only time he would open his mouth was to "*correct*" us or punish us.

And then, when I was about 9 years, old my father tried to rape me. If you've never been exposed to anything like this before (on television, through gossip, discussions, or knowledge otherwise) this kind of situation is shocking to your system, to say the least. Up to this point I had only been on this planet for 9 years and I had never known of anything called "*sexual abuse.*"

You don't know understand what's happening, at the time that it's happening. You don't realize that this is "*attempted rape,*" when you're going through it.

All I knew is that I was outside playing with my friends one Saturday morning, while my mother was at work, and my father called me into the house. He picked me up, took my shorts and my panties off, sat me on the bathroom counter, sprayed shaving cream around my genitals (not sure why), and then tried to stick his penis inside of me.

It wasn't until the very moment that he exposed his penis that I even realized anything "*wrong*" was happening. I have never experienced anything "*inappropriate*" with my dad before this moment, so I didn't think anything of it, as weird as it felt... it didn't feel "*wrong.*"

Until he exposed his penis, and tried to stick it inside of me.... and I **FREAKED THE FUCK OUT**. And I'm talking... **FLIPPED OUT ON HIM.** Mostly out of shock, I think.

I just started screaming, "Dad, what are you doing, what are you doing, what are you doing?" And I yelled for my brother. "*Ssshhhhh*," he urged me to quit making so much noise. He finally stopped and tried to calm me down, but I managed to squeeze away and I took off running.

And I ran... and I ran... and I ran... all the way down the street to an old abandoned house. I literally just sat there in the corner of a dark and empty room, all alone, until the sun went down.

THE STRIPPING OF MY INNOCENCE

I've heard recently that the number of children who actually stand up to child abuse (especially sexual abuse) is about .01%. Not sure if that statistic is true or not, but I am one of those kids. How? I have no idea. All I can do is look back with gratitude for my unknown ability to say "NO."

Still, the fear and shock that goes into your body when you experience something like this is nothing I can explain with words. It's debilitating in the moment. It's unfamiliar. I still, to this day, cannot seem find the correct language to aptly clarify the emotional trauma one faces in this moment.

The first time anyone attempts to sexually assault you, you endure a mind fuck like you can't imagine.

And then, to make it even more of a mind fuck for me... my dad, a week later, cornered me in the kitchen, one afternoon, and actually said these words to me: *"I can't make love to you even though I know you want me to. It's not fair to your mom."*

This is what a 40-year-old father said to his 9-year-old daughter. Just take a moment here and really grasp this reality. Imagine a 40-year-old man you know, and picture any 9-year-old kid, and imagine this conversation taking place between the two of them.

The reality of this moment for me was so unfathomable I was in just as much shock as I was at the original offense. I was completely taken aback, and taken off guard.

However, there was something strangely healing in this moment for me too. Because in this very moment, with this epically crazy conversation, where my 40 year old father is telling me he can't *"make love to me,"* it also instantly hit me that this man is not only sick, he's also fucking crazy.

Liiiiike...bat-shit crazy!

See, up until this moment, I remember being so angry with myself, feeling as though the attempted rape that Saturday morning was my fault.

I so badly wanted to be a "*daddy's girl,*" that perhaps I had been too affectionate? I shouldn't have asked to sit on his lap last weekend when we watched a movie. I should never have told him I loved him. I shouldn't have asked to sit next to him at church last Sunday.

I remember actually thinking these thoughts, as a young child. Was this my fault? Did I cause this?

But the moment I'm hearing my dad explain he can't make love to me because, "*It's not fair to my mother...*" I walked away from that moment realizing this isn't my fault.

The look on my face was total shock. I stuttered back... reluctantly, and uncomfortably.... "*Um...okay*" is all I could think to say. Then I ran off.

Then, about two weeks later I woke up to him standing over my bed while I was sleeping. He was masturbating. I literally didn't know what to do, so I submerged my body completely underneath my covers. I just laid there motionless until he finished and left.

No one in my family understood why, but after the first attack, I asked my little sister if she'd like to share a room with me. She, of course, was ecstatic to stay in the same place as her bigger sister. My mom agreed. And, my sister and I moved in together.

I look back on these moments with total shock and gratitude. How I had composed myself enough to just *"make a plan of survival"* to mitigate as many *"crazy outbreak episodes"* as possible is beyond my comprehension. I was just a kid. But **GOOD LORD** my *"survival skills"* were off the chain (if I do say so myself).

INSTANT SURVIVAL SKILLS

THESE WERE THE RULES I LIVED BY IN MY HOME:

1. Move into the same room as my little sister.
2. Do not come home until my mom is present. (this was important because my dad always came home from work one hour before my mom every day).
3. Stay away from him as much as possible.
4. Never go anywhere alone with him.
5. Never be alone in the same room with him.
6. Never look him directly in the eyes. This was my biggest fear, as somehow I translated *"looking him directly in the eyes"* to think he would interpret it as some kind of invitation to assault me.

So my little sister and I moved in together because I assumed that if we were sharing a room, he was less likely to attempt to assault me at night again.

However, it never stopped him from standing over my bed and masturbating. This incident happened a dozen times as a child – waking up abruptly to the sound of my father masturbating over my bed. Watching me sleep. Each and every time, I would submerge myself underneath the covers and hide until I heard him walk away.

The incessant attempts to sexually abuse me actually never ended. I had a sleepover one night when I was 11. Five of my friends and I were sleeping in the living room, all in our individual sleeping bags. In the middle of the night, he literally pulled my sleeping bag out of the living room and attempted to lay on top of me. I screamed, and he jumped off of me and ran into the bedroom. My friend woke up and said, "*Why are you all the way in the hallway?*" I slept in her sleeping bag with her for the rest of the night.

He was never successful. And, he never tried actually raping me again. He would just do things like show me his genitals or masturbate around me.

However, as with most abusers... he started getting more and more angry... more and more out of control... and more and more creative with how he could abuse me.

The fear of abuse every single day of my life was far more emotionally traumatizing than the abuse itself in many ways. It was a constant overwhelming feeling that I lived with my entire life. It was like I was constantly being chased in a dark forest against a monster, of whom I had no defense.

When would he try it again? What's next?

I spent the majority of my childhood with him staring at me through some unsuspecting window somewhere. He'd tell me I needed to change clothes for no reason at all, simply so he could try to catch a glimpse of me naked.

I would be bathing and he would come to tell me it was time to get out of the bathtub, and then just stand there in the doorway of the bathroom until I stood up to get out.

One time he asked if he could watch me clean my *"private area,"* and my mom walked in and asked what he was doing. He said he was just making sure I was taking a good bath, and then she walked out. I felt like I was screaming inside to get her attention and she never once looked my way.

I remember I used to stand in the doorway of my mother's room while she was getting ready for bed... these words were screaming in my mind, *"He's abusing me, please, please help me."* But I couldn't say it.

As I stood there, she would often say, *"What do you want? Spit it out, or go away."* ... and away I would go without saying a word...

THE DETOUR

The ultimate breaking point for me was when he became so agitated over his inability to sexually abuse me that he started to physically abuse me, in an unsuspecting *"sexual"* way.

When had the desire to *"beat"* me, instead of just *"beating me"* like any other asshole would beat their kid, he would make me take off my pants and sometimes strip down naked.

I can't define the feelings inside of me, nor find any corresponding words to reflect the anger seething through a child when her father, who has been trying to abuse her sexually (but can't), starts to use physical abuse as a means to sexually assault.

However, out of all this craziness... if I could pick out one single incident that caused the rage inside of me to grow the most, it would be the time that he said he was going to spank me and he mandated that I take off all of my clothes. When I refused to do so, my mother told me to take off my pants and my panties, so he could hit me... and (in her words), *"Just let him get this over with."*

I can't even explain to you what I felt in that moment.

I can't say the word *"betrayal"* because that word doesn't define the act against me from my own mother – as my father looks at me with the smirk on his face, while I'm forced to undress in front of him.

Rage isn't right. Anger isn't enough. Sadness doesn't even begin to define the top layer of a mountain of incomprehensible emotions storming within me.

I had spent years running and fighting and hiding and defending myself....and in this one moment, I stood powerless as my own mother asked me to do what my abuser needed me to do, simply so that he could get his dick hard while he was beating the fucking shit out of me.

... so he could get his dick hard while he was beating the fucking shit out of me.

Do I think she knew? No chance. I think she thought if she didn't appease him, however, that it would create chaos. And I think she would do anything she could to keep the peace – including mandating that I undress so that he could literally beat me while having an erotic moment doing it.

He never hit her.
He never hit my sister.
As far as I recall he never ever even punished my sister.
But he was like a raging alcoholic who never needed alcohol to rage when it came to my brother and myself.

SIR, ARE YOU ABUSING YOUR CHILDREN?

The abuse started growing so obvious in our home that someone on our street actually called the authorities. And... totally, unexpectedly (out of the blue) one Saturday morning, waltzed in two of the world's most epically, fucking stupid social workers to our home.

I call them *"epically fucking stupid"* because these two women **LITERALLY** came into our home and said the words, *"We have received a report that there is possible abuse happening in this home. So we would like to gather the entire family together to discuss this."*

Wait... Hold the phone...
UM. WHAT?

Did you just tell me that you're going to ask us about the abuse in our home **IN FRONT OF THE MAN WHO IS ACTUALLY ABUSING US?**

How in the fuck did you land this job?

I will literally never forget this woman who was sitting next to my dad, as my dad (who was sitting directly across from me) asked me if I am being abused by anyone in my home.

I just started stuttering... I was actually just in shock, by the blob of stupidity in front of me, so much so that I was just sitting there shaking my head in disbelief. My brother and I just kept looking at each other, shaking our heads... as the words failed to come out of our mouths.

Then this woman jokingly turned to my dad and says, *"Sir, are you abusing your children?"* He just chuckled, albeit somewhat nervously, and said, *"No,"* which she does not pick up on.

The woman eventually just says, "Well, I think everything looks pretty great here. You guys have a lovely home. If you need me just give me a call," **AND THEN SHE TURNS AROUND AND HANDS MY DAD HER CARD.**

I mean... holy fucking mother fucker fucking **FUCKING** shit!!!

Dear Social Worker:
I feel like this little *"The More You Know"* section should go without saying, but let me just say it anyway: Please do not be so brazenly ignorant as to walk into any home where there has been suspicion of abuse and ask any child in front of any parent, ever, for the truth.

MY HERO

Six months after this moment, my brother and I were alone together and he asked me if there was anything going on between dad and me.

"*What do you mean?*" I asked.
"*Like.... has he ever tried to touch your privates or anything?*" He asked.
"*Why would you ask me this?*" I asked.
"*Because he tried doing it to me not too long ago, and I swear to God I would fucking kill him if I found out he ever did this to you.*" He said.

So I shared with him all that had been happening to me, and before I could even get 30 seconds into this conversation he rushed down the stairs, went rummaging through my dad's closet, found his gun, walked into the living room where both of our parents were sitting (quietly watching television), and pointed the gun at my father's head, saying, "*If you ever touch my little sister again, I will fucking kill you.*"

I was watching the entire scene play out while peeking through the staircase, in between the stairs. I remember thinking, "*Holy fuck, my brother is a badass... and a little crazy.*" My mother instantly jumped to my father's defense. "*What are you talking about Scott?*"

My brother told her what I had shared with him. Suddenly, my dad burst into tears, and my mother marched straight up the stairs and said these words to me: "*Do you hear your dad downstairs crying? Do you hear that? You did that to him. How could you accuse him of doing something like this to you? He loves you, and he would never do that to you. You need to go downstairs and apologize to him right now.*"

I remember standing there, staring her in the eyes, and I said, *"No. I will never apologize to him. Beat me, slap me, ground me, kill me... I will never apologize to him."*

She told me I could stay in my room for the night and think about what I've done.

And I did. I thought about it all night long... and all day long... and all month long... and all year long... and my life long through...

But I didn't think about what I had done. I thought about what **SHE JUST DID TO ME.**

SIGNS OF ABUSE

Please never dismiss a child who is trying to cry out for help. The signs aren't always obvious. It's imperative that you watch and you listen, and you pay close attention. Let me give you some obvious signs that can illuminate potential abuse happening in your home.

- When a kid suddenly changes behavior towards any adult in the home.
- When a kid suddenly does things for *"protection"* in your home.
- When a kid's personality changes drastically.
- When their grades in school drop for no reason.
- When they start to become isolated from friends or other family.
- When they refuse to suddenly participate in family activities, or activities with adults around.
- When their physical appearance suddenly and/or drastically changes.
- When they keep trying to tell you something, over and over, but can't seem to find the right words.

There are many more, but these were the signs I displayed in our home; and looking back I realize that had anyone just been paying attention, even just a little bit, they would have seen the obvious.

I have replayed the moment my mother asked me to go apologize to my dad over and over and over in my mind, and I've considered the reality of this experience and what it ultimately did to me growing up.

Being sexually violated is a gross injustice, **YES**. It definitely fucks you up in the head. But being dismissed when you're literally crying for help.... now **THAT** is something that will actually cause you to want to put a bullet in your own head.

I felt... in that moment, in my life, that the innocence in me left my heart.

The world suddenly felt different. Life would no longer be the same for me. Hate, resentment and anger ruled my life for the next fifteen years after this moment.

A SUM OF THE CONTINUED CHAOS

My mid teens just looked like a clusterfuck of insanity.

Chaos ensued because suddenly my rage turned into action... and I started becoming wildly defiant, destructive, and depressed.

I started running away.
I started skipping school.
I started smoking cigarettes.
I hotwired a car once, just to see if I could. Then I started driving around the parking lot because I didn't have anywhere to go... I just wanted to do something wrong.

At this point in my childhood, I was convinced that the only way to get anyone's attention was by doing things I wasn't supposed to do.

One of the most difficult things I've had to work through is the anger, resentment and betrayal I have felt over my mother throughout this whole thing.

It seemed bad enough, to me, that she never protected me or never stopped to listen to me; but the night my brother confronted my dad, she never even bothered asking me **WHY** I said what I said.

And to add salt to a **VERY LARGE, OPEN,** and **DEEPLY-PAINFUL** wound, she started ridiculing me for my defiance. And... to this very day, she seems to take great pleasure in telling people how bad I was as a child, without sharing with them why.

She told me that she wrote a book once. One of the chapters was "*1/3 odds aren't bad*" – meaning... at least 1 out of her 3 kids turned out okay... As if to dismiss everything I had ever been through in my life, at the hands of her own husband... As if to say, "*I know your sister was never abused as you were, but at least she didn't turn out to be someone who embarrasses me.*"

I spent my life angrier with my mom than my dad. The disloyalty and betrayal from her felt deeper. It felt deeper because I witnessed her being a great mom to my little sister, so I know it was possible. I knew she had it in her. I never witnessed my dad abusing my sister, but I also never witnessed him being a good dad. So, it all just felt "impersonal". As sad as it was to not have a father I had hoped for, neither did either of my siblings, therefore... it's a reality of my life I just had to come to terms with.

But my mom was a different story. She was a great mom to my little sister. She formed such a loving, affectionate, close relationship with her that I watched from a distance with jealousy, pain and confusion.

And so I tried to constantly get her attention. I tried to the good route. I tried the great route. I tried the "*attention*" route. I tried the route of total defiance. I tried the cool route.

I took piano lessons, and I was extremely good at it. Yet, no one cared. I got the lead role in my high school musicals. No one cared. I learned to play 9 different instruments. No one cared. I landed the solo in my national choir contest. No one cared. I took my city softball team to state. No one cared.

In fact, I played softball for 5 years throughout my childhood, and my mother (to this day) has never seen me play.

I tried to be someone she could be proud of and it never seemed to matter.

The truth is... I know that she was only focusing on my little sister because that was the one thing that she didn't feel like a failure with. I know that she could be proud of herself, at least, if my sister turned out to be okay.

I definitely understood why... but it never mitigated the pain within me that longed for her acceptance and affection.

When I realized that getting lead roles in musicals, learning to dance, playing instruments, being good at sports and being popular in school wasn't going to be good enough, I tried the route that every other broken kid takes... I defied all authority and I practiced the art of rebellion... like I was going for the gold.

No one ever questioned why...

THERE IS NEVER A CHANGE OF BEHAVIOR WITHOUT FIRST A CHANGE OF CIRCUMSTANCES.

If you truly love your children, do not beat them down for any behavior problems you feel they are exhibiting. Instead, love them enough to find out why. There is never a change in behavior without a change in circumstance preceding it.

No kid actually **WANTS** to get into trouble. **NO KID.**

MY BROTHER'S BREAKING MOMENT

One morning as we were all getting ready for school, my brother excitedly took the shared calendar on our fridge and highlighted his high school graduation day. "YAY," he wrote, and drew a heart around it. It was literally only three months away at that point.

My dad, being the douche-canoe that he was, came in right after him and wrote the words, "*As if you'll ever be good enough to ever graduate from anything.*"

I remember my mom standing in the kitchen watching my father do this and just saying, "*James...*" as if she needed to let him know she didn't approve, but didn't quite have it in her to stop him.

And I will **NEVER** forget sitting at the kitchen bar and seeing the look on my brother's face when he saw what my dad had done. It was such a sadness that fell over him... a sadness that had finally been overcome by defeat.

That morning my brother quit school and ran away from home. I didn't see him for almost a whole year.

SILENCE ISN'T NEUTRAL

I think it's imperative that you understand that if your spouse is abusing your children and you refuse to acknowledge it, your silence is being translated as acceptance, and that acceptance makes you a co-conspirator of abuse. And your need for reconciliation and a full acceptance of responsibility will look almost identical to theirs in the end.

If you have experienced this position, I would strongly encourage you to begin your journey of responsibility and reconciliation by offering a full apology that begins with acknowledgment.

Healing can begin earlier for kids of abuse when the abuse is first acknowledged by those who participated, whether directly or indirectly.

It's never too late to do what you should have done.
It's never too late to be what you could have been.

HAVE YOU EVER HEARD OF THE ELEPHANT - ROPE SYNDROME?

Did you know that when baby elephants are captured in the wild they are immediately chained down with thick, steel chains around their ankles or necks to teach them that they cannot escape? Here's the **crazy** part.

As the elephant grows bigger, and much stronger, it actually needs **LESS** chain to keep it captive, not more.

It's called the Baby Elephant Rope Syndrome. Even though the elephants grow significantly stronger than the chains that bind them, they don't even try to escape, simply because they have been conditioned to believe they cannot. In fact, often times these chains are replaced with mere rope, wrapped around their ankles, as a simple reminder of their captivity.

At any moment they could break free... but their perception of reality will keep them forever enslaved.

... and here's the crazier part.

You're no different from these adult elephants ... You've been conditioned too. We all have.

Let me prove that point to you right now.

The truth is that you could make a million dollars within the next couple of years. You could fall madly in love with the love of your life. You could find a dream career that makes you feel like you will never have to work a day in your life. You could leave it all behind and find epic happiness like you've never known before, living in overwhelming abundance, surrounded by love, kindness, opportunities, hope, and wealth. And the only reason that you don't live like this is because you don't believe it's possible. You are like the elephant, standing in the middle of your own life with this tiny little thread wrapped around your mind. Standing there...as if you don't have a choice otherwise...

Someone somewhere along the way told you that you "*aren't good enough,*" that "*you'll never be pretty enough or talented enough,*" that "you'll never have more or be more than you have now." And you believed these words...and that belief has been like a chain wrapped around you in life, precluding you from epic greatness. You've been conditioned to believe that **THIS** is all that life has to offer you... and so you stay here, as if those words were true.

Those words weren't real. You've always been free... free to be, to have, to experience, to live life on a level that you've always dreamed of. You've always been enough. Actually you've always been more than enough.

REMOVE THE CHAINS

THE WORDS YOU SPEAK BECOME THE HOUSE YOU LIVE IN

Words are powerful, and they needlessly bind us to people, places, and things that aren't as strong as we are.

You are beautiful. You are perfectly, exactly as you should be in this moment. And there is only one you on this entire planet...and it is your responsibility to bring to the table of life **THAT WHICH YOU WERE SENT HERE TO BRING.**

Here are the conditions I believed in, coming out of my childhood. These were the chains binding me...

I can't trust anyone!
No one truly loves me.
No one will ever protect me.
No one thinks I'm "*good enough.*"
I'm not "*good enough.*"
I deserve to be discarded.
I am an epic disappointment.
I'm not smart.
I'm not pretty.
I am not good for anything other than sex and sexual acts.
I should be ashamed that I was adopted.
Adopted kids aren't as good as "*real*" kids.
I will never become anything worthy of anyone caring.

The best thing about me is my sense of humor.
THIS I WAS TOLD OFTEN (and kind of agree with).

So... what does a kid like me, who grew up like this and learned these lessons, do with all of this?

I go on a freaking rampage as an adult... I act as destructively as humanly freaking possible.

I flip old ladies off at the grocery store (I actually did that once, for no reason at all).
I steal things I don't even need or want (just to say, "*fuck you*" to the authority that didn't catch me).
I use people for their money.
I lie.
I abuse people's time.
I cheat on everyone I'm ever with.
I refuse to ever be on time, for anything... because I got some total head rush to show people I am in control, not them.
I never keep my promises.
I rarely do anything, if ever, for anyone but myself.
I become wildly promiscuous as a teenager.

And, I basically spent my entire 20's angry, sad and on the verge of a complete suicidal meltdown if the freaking wind blew into my hair wrong.

KIDS… WE'RE GOING TO DISNEYLAND…

JUST KIDDING, WE'RE GETTING DIVORCED

When I was 16 years old, my little sister and I were on our way to go play tennis, and our dad passed us in the hallway and said (as casually and flippantly as you can imagine), "*Mom and I are getting divorced. I'm moving out to go live with Grandma and Grandpa.*"

My sister and I just looked at each other, and then looked at him and said, "*Okay.*" Then we left for the tennis court, and I only saw my dad one more time in my lifetime from that moment.

WHAT IN THE HELL DID YOU JUST SAY TO ME?

Later that night I saw my mom sitting out on our back patio and I sat down next to her to discuss what was going on.

"*What made you decide to get divorced all of a sudden? Why now?*" I asked.

Her immediate response was something I will never in my life forget, as it became the ultimate catalyst of the breaking moment between us.

"*I've been going to counseling with Brother Bobby over this at the church. I know it's a sin to divorce your husband, but I can't do it anymore. Plus, one time when you were younger and we were living at the other house, my friend, Sharon, said to me that she was worried about you because she thought you seemed to act very peculiar any time your dad was in the room. She thought I should check into whether or not he was abusing you. And I just never did it. I couldn't make myself do anything about it. But now, I just don't want to deal with it anymore.*"

I went into an absolute fit of rage and anger and (yes) disobedience. For the first time in my life, I yelled at my mom.

"NEVER are you allowed to say that you are getting divorced for me. If you were ever going to do anything for me, you should have done it 9 years ago when I was being chased through our home and I literally shit my pants with terror because I was fucking afraid of what he was going to do to me if he caught me. And now you say that you want to protect me? Now that you can't personally handle him anymore and you want a divorce?"

So, anyway... I hated my mom...

MY LIFE FELL APART OFFICIALLY

(Here's a sum of the next two years in 2 pages)

At this point in my life I hated everyone, but mostly myself.

I quit high school.

I got a stupid job, with this crappy company that sold hydroponic systems. I was told they were for indoor gardening enthusiasts who wanted to enjoy freshly grown tomatoes all year long. I was so clueless and careless, that actually made sense to me.

I was like, *"Yes, tomatoes... all year.... sounds delicious."*
I was partying. I started drinking and smoking.

I started nude modeling for money.
I ended up pregnant a few months later.
Ended up homeless a few months after that.

So... naturally, now I hate even more people.
I hate everyone who isn't homeless, basically.
I wrecked my car.
I lost my job.

I took all of the rage within me... and I destroyed myself with it.

I gave birth to my son, got into an epic court battle for custody of him, lost custody of him (which is a whole other book in itself)...

I tried to commit suicide... a few times...

I got caught stealing, I went to jail.
I tried to kill myself again...

... and I eventually (accidentally) found myself in therapy... (golf clap) yaaaay...

Therapy couldn't have come at a better time for me. Because by this point, I had lost it. I was gone. I was literally stripped away from existence and felt like a shell, walking on this earth.

The slightest thing that could possibly go wrong would cause me to entertain suicidal thoughts.

I was always on the verge of suicide...

I started crying once because I couldn't find a parking space at the beach. And I didn't even really want to go to the beach... I just wanted to sit there and stare at the ocean.

But I couldn't find a place to do that... and **THAT FUCKING PARKING SPACE WAS SOMEHOW SYMBOLIC OF EVERY DISAPPOINTMENT IN MY LIFE.**

I reacted the exact same way to not being able to find a parking space as I did when I realized I was 7-months pregnant and didn't have any place to sleep one night.

I ran out of gas.
I lost my son.
I have no place to sleep.
7-11 is out of Cheesy Doritos.
My dad just masturbated over my bed.

I reacted the same in all of these situations because they all just brought out the rage that consumed me.

Rage is rage.
Anger is anger.
Sadness is sadness.
And brokenness is just brokenness.

I'll never forget walking to this therapist's office and saying to her, "*I don't know why I am here. I don't have any issues to work through.*"

I'll just cut straight to the chase with this one... needless to say, I had some "*issues*" to work through.

I mean... you know... just a couple...

I saw her 3 times a week for 3 years.
And I began processing all of the above...

THERAPY IS AWESOME…

AND IT'S EXTREMELY DESTRUCTIVE.

The first thing this therapist taught me… was to be insanely pissed. It was okay. I was trying so hard to hide my rage, and she taught that there's no reason for that.

It felt amazing to be able to sit and share my stories. It felt good just to get all of this OUT of me. I literally felt like there was this demon inside of me called "*my childhood*," and I just wanted it to be free.

But let me be very candid here… Therapy was also one of the biggest catalysts that gave me permission to be even more destructive than I already had been.

THERAPY CAN BE AS DANGEROUS AS IT IS HELPFUL.

My therapist excused all of my bad behavior. Chalked it all up to "*the abuse I endured, which clearly caused me to act out.*" She removed fault from me, and she basically offered me a golden ticket to continue to be as selfishly destructive as I could be… because life had been so unfair to me that I deserved to give back some of that yuckiness.

I mean, she didn't "*say*" that necessarily, but it was certainly implied by the lack of personal responsibility she ever expressed I should take. Literally NOTHING was my fault.

(PART 3)

THE RECKONING

A FAREWELL TO MY HERO

My brother ended up dying of a really rare blood disease about four years ago, when he was only 39 years old. It was officially the most epically difficult moment of my life. He and I had continued to remain close as adults, so you can imagine the pain I felt, having lost this person who felt so much a part of me my entire life.

However, his death brought me to my knees in a way I had never experienced before. It shattered me in a way I had never known. And, that experience brought a significant and difficult reality before me.

The reality is that if we do not work on the hard stuff within us, it will only compound and continue to grow like an insidious disease, until it gradually and suddenly kills us. Emotional trauma can be just as significant as physical trauma. However, unlike the physical trauma that we can see, emotional trauma can be a silent killer that slowly begins to break our lives down, piece by piece.

Emotional trauma can kill your marriage, all of your relationships and your careers. It can kill your ability to maintain a healthy lifestyle. And, it will eventually eradicate all senses of balance within you.

> After a lifetime of ignored emotional trauma, you come to the overwhelming conclusion that you just can't handle any of it anymore. And if it hasn't killed you yet, at this point, you start to contemplate suicide.

This is where I was after my brother died. I just wanted to kill myself (again). Again, as I had wanted to when I was a kid as I stood inside a store one afternoon asking my dad if I could buy a new pair of hair barrettes, to which he replied, "Only if you do something back for me when we get home."

They were fifty-cent hair barrettes that he was now using to barter my innocence with. The fucking anger and sadness that seethed through me in that moment finally ended with a conclusion that this could all end if I could just be strong enough to kill myself.

And the moment Scott died it all came rushing back through me, only this time it was far more out of control than anything I had ever felt before. This was a whole new level of pain that I had never experienced before.

I realized instantly, as I was holding my brother in my arms as he passed away, that I had spent a lifetime living life with open wounds all over my body, exposed to all of the elements.

This is why the pain tingles when the wind blows.

And this is why it eventually becomes too daunting in the end. I was faced with an overwhelming reality that I had never dealt with any of the emotional trauma within me. I had only, up to this point, "talked about the trauma in therapy." And there's a significant difference between "talking" and "*healing*." Talking is only a small part of the healing process; and if it ends there, it will all just stay there.

I become angry suddenly at the reality that therapy never helped me in any capacity.

THERAPY DIDN'T HELP ME GROW:
It helped me become self-destructive.
It helped me stay in a space of "human ego."
It helped me create excuses.
It helped me become more entitled.

And it wasted a space in my life when I should have been growing. Instead I spent it stagnant.

Twelve years later, from the last time I saw my therapist is when my brother died, I finally shattered into pieces in a way that I had no single fragment to glue anything back together to. It was the final breaking point for me.

Yes, death is an enormously painful experience all in itself. However, even death shouldn't break you down to an unrecognizable reality. The truth is that the only thing that has the power to do this is a lifetime of unanswered hurt, brought to a single moment of truth before you.

If anything can break you down to this level, it wasn't "that thing" that broke you; it was a conglomeration of it all within you. It wasn't about the death, it was about the accumulation of pain within me.
The reality was that I still had a LOT of work to do.

I think this is an important part of my journey because I think THIS truth may be one of the greatest truths that help get others back on track.

> **THERE IS A SIGNIFICANT DIFFERENCE BETWEEN "GOING" THROUGH SOMETHING AND "GROWING" THROUGH SOMETHING.**

The reality of who I had become, where I was in life, and how I had gotten there had never seem more obvious than the moment my brother passed away in my arms. We are truly only as strong as our weakest links within us.

THIS is ultimately when my responsibility began... I had a lot of things I needed to take responsibility for... starting with the fact that I hadn't yet actually dealt with any of this pain inside of me.

I never worked through anything.
I never grew up.
I never changed.
I never discovered epic truths within myself.
I never came to the conclusion that maybe, just maybe I had taken all of the bad that had been done to me, and I had chosen to become equally as bad?

THE MOMENT TRUTH HITS YOU IN THE FACE

I think therapy is a really interesting thing. It logically makes sense that it would be good for you, as I did, to get that shit out of your head.

But you have to be very mindful of what's happening. I actually thought for a moment I was getting worse. I was becoming angrier, and I certainly wasn't "*processing*" anything, because all she ever did was coddle me and cater to my emotions.

There was no discussion of personal responsibility. There was no "*growth.*" There was only me, my rage, my stories, and the excuses that I was now allowed to give myself.

She once told me not to be too hard on myself because I told her that I felt kind of guilty about sleeping with my boss, Kim, who was married to my other boss, Stewart.

Really? Don't be too hard on myself?
I was just thinking that it's wrong to sleep with married people... but cool. Thanks for the golden ticket to infidelity and lacking even the slightest modicum of morality. COOL.

Everything got talked about but nothing ever really got worked out. I spent three years in therapy with her. I went a lot and she literally never discussed anything that I maybe could have done to have contributed to the epic shit my life kept finding itself in. Nothing, literally was ever my fault.

IS YOUR THERAPIST TRULY HELPING?

I think it is wildly imperative that IF you are in therapy that you are willing to be extremely honest with yourself in this moment and ask yourself "is this therapist truly helping me discover truths, no matter how difficult, that are leading me to responsibility and growth, or is this therapist coddling me and keeping me in a space of complacency, where my ego is being fed and not my spirit?"

Do you leave therapy feeling justified for all of your thoughts and behaviors? Or do you leave therapy with a clear plan of action for change and a new perspective towards healing?

You need to be making progress. If you've been in therapy for a solid year and you're still depressed, or still feeling as lost as you were when you first walked in, you should consider finding a new therapist.

After all, in the end, healing is about letting go, not figuring out how to continue to hold on, and live "around the pain."

It's also important for you to understand that the Western Therapy Model is not the only option for healing. There are healers, and teachers, and meditations, and healing sources you can also discover. And, of course, not all therapists are the same.

Keep knocking until someone who answers the door can bring you back home.

WHY TAKE RESPONSIBILITY...
ESPECIALLY WHEN NO ONE IS EXPECTING YOU TO?

The truth is that **IT IS EASY TO BLAME** those around us when we have legitimate stories in our past that coincide with living in chaos in your future.

"**OF COURSE** *you stole things, Kristy... you were abused by your father. You were adopted. You never felt loved. You were abandoned in life. You had it rough growing up. You poor thing...*"

I heard it all, and I accepted it all as truth. I soaked up all of the excuses I could, simply so that I didn't have to take any personal responsibility for what had happened to my life.

But here's the problem... excuses only prolong the pain.

Excuses only prolong the pain. They are a way to sweep it all under the rug, until of course one day someone pulls that rug out from underneath you and what you will discover is a lifelong history of pain that was never dealt with. And unlike every other time you've been able to turn your back on yourself (and pretend as though you're fine), you'll be faced with a great mirror that only reflects all that you have been disregarding. There will be a reckoning some day where you will be faced with the truth.

"THE ANSWER TO THE PAIN IS INSIDE THE PAIN." - RUMI

It's being able to stare at your pain, head on, and looking it square in the eyes, and say *"What do you want from me?"*

Let me tell you... it's freaking hard – but it's freaking worth it!

Deep breathe. It was hard to accept that I created all of the chaos and dissidence. I quit high school. I got myself pregnant. I put myself in a situation where I couldn't even take care of my own kid. I became homeless all on my own. I made these decisions. I chose every action. I chose every reaction. I mindfully participated in living my life.

THE BULLSHIT STORIES WE SPIN
TO DEAL WITH OUR PAIN....

We've all done it. Added little twists to the stories, so we don't feel so bad about our decisions. Pretended like we are the innocent victims in a hateful world of scammers and schemers, all trying to rape us of our innocence.

The lies we call "*misinterpretations.*" The "*accidents*" we continue to repeat. All manipulative tactics we use on ourselves, and **ALL ONLY** to avoid the pain within us.

I used to tell people I quit high school because my parents got divorced and they forced me to work. **TOTAL BULLSHIT.** I was lazy, and I had no logical understanding of the ramifications of not having a high school diploma.

I used to tell people I got pregnant because a much older man coerced me into sex...and "*that one time*" I got pregnant. **TOTAL BULLSHIT.** I dated my son's father for months before getting pregnant.

I found myself homeless and pregnant and penniless; suicidal and hopeless at the age of 17 and **I COULD NOT** (for the **LIFE OF ME**) accept the responsibility of my own actions. The reality of what I had done to my own life was overwhelming.

It was a burden too great to carry, because the consequences were too much for me to accept. So I continued to lie and make excuses and search for all of the reasons in life that all of the **SHIT** was never my fault.

No, it wasn't my fault that I was abused; but it was my fault that I used that abuse as an excuse to not walk in the light, or chose to ignore the convictions of my own character or morality.

There are a lot of people on this planet growing up without love... but they didn't turn to a life of crime and disdain for authority. That was my choice.

There are all kinds of people who grew up abused... and they didn't turn to lying and stealing and cheating.... **THAT WAS MY CHOICE.**

I spent most of my life thinking I hated everyone around me... until I finally realized one day that it wasn't them I hated... it was **ME.** I epically hated myself for taking every bad thing that had happened **TO** me and turning it into something bad **FOR** me, within me.

I took my dad's craziness, and I became **crazy.** I adopted my mom's emotional apathy towards those in my life, and I became distant from the world around me. I took it all in... and I gave it all right back out. In a different way, I had become as bad as those who I felt had wronged me. Where is the justice in that?

This is the cycle of our pain that we continue to cultivate and pass on to one another and our children.

I think it's important to note that if you ignore the pain within you, you will pass it on to your children, as my dad did to me.

The ultimate reality of my responsibility goes as deep to say that, because I had accepted his pain as my own and became his pain in my own way, I am glad that I was not in the position to raise my son as I had fought to do.

My responsibility has led me to the truth that I needed to heal the hurt within me before I could truly build deep, meaningful relationships, including that with my own child. This was an extraordinarily difficult truth that led to another piece of the freedom puzzle for me.

There is **NOTHING** more liberating than taking responsibility for it all... because from there you grow, you learn how to forgive yourself. You learn how to love yourself again.

What is the single most difficult thing about your life that you, up until now, have not been able to face with an honest reflection?

I HAVE TO BECOME BETTER THAN THE HURT.

The instant realization I had when I started contemplating writing another book is that if I don't take true responsibility, I will have actually become my mother. And my 4mother, and her refusal to accept responsibility for anything, is what broke me the most as a child.

She always used to say to me, *"Sometimes it's just easier to keep your head in the sand."* I agree. I 100% agree, it's definitely easier.

But what I know about life is that I don't want to face this level of pain again. I want to grow through it, so I don't have to go through it all over a 2nd time. I also know that taking responsibility for the people we've hurt, for the things we've said, for the actions committed against ourselves and others – this is the space where truth and freedom lie.

I used to wonder if my mom ever worried about me. If she ever felt guilty. If she ever wondered how I was doing. I used to wonder if she ever wished she would have held me or played with my hair and told me she loved me. Or did she just constantly regret having adopted me at all?

The truth is now that I actually don't believe my mom thinks about me at all.

Because, like Chicken Man, to think about me would be to consider a reality far too difficult to accept. It would be to contemplate the reality that someone warned her that they believed her 9-year-old daughter was probably getting abused, and she chose to ignore it. She cannot come to the truth that I was left alone, barely able to even understand any of this life we live, and was being haunted by this man who kept stealing my innocence from me.

I remember being 10 years old and I got this really cool new bike for Christmas. It was purple and had this ridiculously long banana seat on it. My dad had to take it out to the garage to do something; and as I'm standing there waiting for him to fix my bike, he tried to take my hand to force me to feel his penis. It's Christmas. I just wanted to ride my new bike.

If there is a single situation, a time-frame in your life, a specific scenario or experience that you refuse to ever look at; a moment in your life you would rather pretend didn't happen, or wasn't real; I can assure you that this is where your greatest opportunities for growth lie.

TREAT YOURSELF HOW YOU WANT TO BE TREATED

I realized that I needed to learn to treat myself in a way that my mom had never treated me. I longed for her to tell me she was proud of me. Instead, I learned to say that to myself.

I used to long for the day when she would tell me she was sorry for it all. Instead, I learned to forgive myself.

I learned to hold myself and offer myself some epic praise for having walked through great fires and never actually bursting into flames.

IF YOU CAN'T CHANGE A SITUATION THEN IT IS THE SITUATION THAT IS SUPPOSED TO CHANGE YOU.

I can't change my mom. I can't force her to "*see*" me, to want to love me more, or offer me affection or kindness. But I know now that it was my responsibility all along to give these things to myself. It was my responsibility to be the hero of my own story.

My mom didn't come into this life to be anything more than the person she was. And I wasn't in her life to have a "*perfect*" relationship from the world's perspective. She and I actually ended up having a "*perfect*" relationship from the perspective of my spiritual growth.

Had my mom been to me what she was to my sister, I would not be writing this book, and you would not be reading these words, and we would not be growing as we are.

YOU CHOSE THIS BEFORE YOU GOT HERE

There are many religions that believe in the concept that we chose the parents we were born into. That we knew that what we needed to learn would be actualized through their own lives, their own suffering, and our experiences with them.

As if to say my mom and dad and I were floating around the cosmos before any of us entered this life and we made an agreement, we created a pact: Okay...you are going to meet me there in this lifetime and you'll play the role of my dad, and you're going to teach me, from a perspective of contrast and duality, about love and truth, freedom and choices, and responsibility. Okay, and you're going to go in as my mom alongside him, and you're going to teach me, also through contrast, all about compassion, consideration, kindness, and forgiveness.

And they both looked at me and said, *"Okay, and you're gong to teach us about patience and kindness and innocence and forgiveness and responsibility."*

And these are the soul pacts that we make with others before coming here. We chose the life we knew would bring us the most growth.

So, if there's any chance that this is true, then it would be the greatest disservice to yourself, and a grave injustice to your spirit, to not choose growth through it all.

AN OFFERING OF ACKNOWLEDGMENT

Before my dad died a few years ago, he reached out to me on Facebook and said, *"I'm having quadruple bypass surgery tomorrow, and just in case something happens to me I just wanted to reach out to you and tell you that I am sorry for not being a better father to you..."*

And **THIS** would have been sufficient...

However the message continued to say, *"But I was dealing with vasectomy issues and so that's why I wasn't always the best."*

I literally cannot even imagine how his having a vasectomy justified years of abuse; however, in some strange way I am at least glad he attempted to reach out to me, with this super-insanely lame excuse.

My response to him:
"I forgave you years ago for the abuse. Your response of 'I had just had a vasectomy' was strange and showed me that you have never actually taken responsibility for your actions, but it's okay because your journey isn't my journey. And I'm not here to judge. I forgave you anyway. What you did to me made me a stronger human being. And in a strange way I feel thankful for that. I certainly wouldn't choose any of it over again, but I am glad I became the woman I did in the end. The truth is that I hope you die happy, and with peace in your heart, and surrounded by those who loved you. I don't know what happens to us when we die, but if your spirit is wandering and lost, I hope it finds a space where it can truly create a new beginning from true peacefulness. I've set you free. Perhaps you can go find my brother out there in the other world and do the same for him. My only prayer for you now is that you truly become a better human in your next life. Until then..."

The truth is that my dad knew that what he had done was wrong. So wrong in fact that he couldn't die without having acknowledged it. However, "*acknowledgment*" and "*responsibility*" are still oceans apart.

One is an admission of truth; the other is an admission of responsibility.

I cannot imagine how difficult it would be to have to come to terms with something of this magnitude, especially as you're facing death.

IF YOU HAVE BEEN AN ABUSER:

Let me urge any of you out there who may be reading this book to please discover this truth for yourself.

Acknowledging what you have done as an abuser will also bring you the level of freedom it has brought me to acknowledge my experience with it.

You CAN be set free in this moment. You CAN find peace. Yes, EVEN YOU can find peace within yourself. It doesn't matter what you've done. There is always space in this life for forgiveness and reconciliation. There will always be a place to heal, and that healing must start within you.

Acknowledge the action. Accept full responsibility. Forgive yourself for what you have done, and begin the healing process.

You will discover a deep, calming element of peace that will begin to erase the suffering within you.

Any of us who have suffered at the hands of an abuser would admit to you right now that we would rather have been the abused than the abuser in this life.

What is before you now is a mountain of guilt, fear, self-loathing, disdain, anger, sadness, and loss that is different than we have suffered.

And there is no abused kid who has had the grace to turn into a self-actualized adult who wouldn't agree with me that we hold space for you to grow in this way.

I hold this space for you right now, that you find the strength to come full term with this. I hold this space for you right now, that you seek enlightenment, that you discover how to forgive, and that you learn to make peace with it all.

And I would also urge you to make peace with those who you have hurt in this way.

Be honest. Stand in truth. Take full responsibility. Acknowledge the pain you have caused. Ask for forgiveness. And begin to move forward in a positive direction.

And remember that their response to your healing has nothing to do with you. Your healing is not tethered to their acceptance of this moment.

They may not be ready to accept it; however, that should not detour you from moving forward on your own.

"What affects you, reflects you."

RELIGIOUS ABUSE

Physical, sexual, emotional, and mental abuse are all extremely difficult to overcome. However, I truly believe that one of the most widely overlooked forms of abuse, that many kids from abused families endure, is also a form of religious abuse.

WHAT IS RELIGIOUS ABUSE?

It's an abuse of the practice of religion itself. It can also be where there's a use of the religious practice to cover the abuse at home, as well as when there is a huge discrepancy between what is being taught in the religion opposed to what is being lived at home.

My family never skipped a single church service – twice on Sundays and every Wednesday night. I spent my summers in church camps, and most of my extra curricular activities were hosted by a church event of some kind.

I cannot explain how spiritually damaging it is to never skip a prayer over a family meal each night, or how challenging it is to watch your dad singing in the choir and praising Jesus the morning after you've just been sexually assaulted by him.

The use of religion to hide abuse is also something that is extremely damaging to one's spiritual growth; and I fear a reality that very few people choose to grow through.

If you have grown up in an abusive environment where there was also a heavy practice of religion, I would encourage you to seek healing, wholeness, and truth in this capacity as well.

You will discover at the end of this book, this is truly where my world started coming back together... with a new understanding of who God was to me and a realization of the abuse suffered in this way.

The ultimate reality, of course, is that my parents and their religious ideologies did not reflect who I discovered God to be. Their religious ideologies were nothing more than a mere adoption of a way to cope with the pain of their own lives.

It's imperative that you end this cycle of abuse in your life, as it is any other type of abuse you may have endured.

(PART 4)

THE HEALING PROCESS

"THE ANSWER TO THE PAIN IS IN THE PAIN." - RUMI

THE SCENE THAT CHANGED IT ALL…

In 2015, I decided to leave my 7.5-year marriage. It was one of the hardest decisions I had ever made. I didn't do it because my ex was a bad person (quite the contrary). I didn't do it because she didn't love me, or because we didn't work well together, or because we were always fighting. None of these things were true.

I left because I realized that she and I had become very immobile together. I did it because I realized that in order for me to grow into the woman who was capable of writing this book, I needed to grow beyond where I had been.

I left because, while there was nothing truly visibly unhealthy about our marriage, there was nothing healthy either. I had become stagnant in life, with someone with whom I was allowing stagnancy to exist, and who offered me the same in return. I realized we had simply spent the greater part of our marriage doing nothing but feeding each other's insecurities, and allowing the bullshit excuses we had always told each other about why we weren't better people, to continue to overrule our internal desires for change. And while we were very much *"synergetic"* in many ways, we were polar opposites in other ways that I could no longer ignore.

Have you ever seen the movie "*Family Man?*" It's one of my all-time favorite movies, ever. In the movie, Nicholas Cage's character falls into a dream where he wakes up the next morning into an entirely new life than the life he has chosen. In the new reality, he's married to his college sweetheart, they have two kids, and he's a tire salesman in New Jersey, working for his father in law. Before the dream he was single, and living as one of the richest men in New York City, on top of the Forbes list of success stories, and lived in the Penthouse apartment of the most expensive building in the city.

There's a scene where he and his wife are shopping at a local mall and he wants to buy a $2,800 suit jacket (because it makes him feel better to wear nice clothing), and they begin arguing about this reality.

And he turns to his wife and he says, "*How could you let me do this? How could you let me become this? I could have been one of the richest men in the world, on top of the Forbes list of success stories. I have to know, Kate, how it is that you allowed me to settle for this life?*"

The point of the movie being that later he realizes that the life he woke up to is far greater than any riches he could acquire otherwise. He begins to slowly see that the love between he and his college sweetheart never wanes; after 13 years of marriage, and 2 kids, and a shitty job, and prosaic life otherwise, they're still unbelievably in love. (You'll have to watch it to see how it ends).

But the point for me is that one single line of "*How could you let me do this. How did you let me become this? I could have been so much greater than this?*"

For some reason, that line really hit me the first time (and the 100th time) I saw it, because it's a reality that I believe is true, in many ways, about relationships (especially your primary relationship you have with a spouse).

Yes, it is imperative that we take personal responsibility for where we are in our lives. However, I believe that it is equally essential that you push one another forward into their greatness, and that you never allow your partner or spouse in life to settle for anything otherwise. It's imperative that you're married to someone who sees what you can become in life, and who reminds you of this truth, especially in the moments that you forget.

My ex and I never pushed one another; emotionally, spiritually, mentally, or otherwise. We had both allowed our wants to masquerade as needs, and neither one of us were doing anything even close to our greatest potential. Quite the opposite, if anything, we were going backwards. We were feeding each other's insecurities, as if we were incapable of change, and allowing one another to create excuses for the lack of growth within us.

I felt as though I had spent the better part of our marriage being broken down by life experiences, (my brother dying, my career in the legal world ending, gaining 50 plus pounds, losing all that I had ever worked for, becoming bankrupt, etc.), and never growing through anything. I felt like I had spent an entire marriage barely surviving life.

When I left the marriage I thought I hated her. In fact, I told her several times that I hated her (certainly something I'm not proud of). But the truth was that I hated who I had become through it all with her (not because of her), and I just couldn't take responsibility for that. I knew that I needed to remove myself from the situation so that I could get a clearer picture of what I had done with my life.
For some reason there was suddenly, in my contemplation of divorce, a deep seeded awareness that I was not living the life I was supposed to be living. My life had been relegated to anything superficial you can imagine that kept me off track from the truth of my purpose.

During our marriage many things happened that broke me down, as I described above; and how we handled these things was so different that it illuminated the core disparities within us. These differences shed a light on great issues that ultimately led to the demise of our relationship.

She grew up Atheist, although grew increasingly admittedly Agnostic, while wanting to raise children who believed it was okay to reject all religious ideologies. Organized religion for me does a grave disservice to our spirits, however I deeply felt connected to a higher power, one that could never even be discussed in my own home.

I instantly realized that my spouse didn't mirror who I wanted to be, or was becoming, she mirrored who I had been. She was a mirror of my past, and all of my insecurities.

I recognized immediately that our relationship had been predicated on serving our ego's, and our fears, and doubts, more than our spirits. Our relationship had been built from a foundation of distrust and fear (more so in ourselves than each other), more than it had hope and respect, and mutual understanding of life.

We both entered broken, and we both stayed holding on to this. This is one way that our marriage felt like it was "*working*," but it wasn't serving either of us. Everything about it felt comfortable, because everything about it felt familiar.

And when you get to a point in your life where you can undeniably say that you know, that you know, that you know that your life has more meaning than the comfort around you, then it becomes impossible to stay where you are.

A CHANCE TO CHANGE IT ALL

For the first time in my life I made a decision to change something significant about my life, without it being forced upon me. For the first time in my life, I had actively chosen to do something outside of my comfort zone, and face my fears.

Each and every time before this that I had considered leaving all I could fixate on is this little 3-year-old in side of me who was tired of feeling abandoned, and was screaming to never be alone, and desperately wanted to belong to something or someone.

She begged me to stay, and so I did.

I would fantasize about leaving my marriage but then I would instantly be brought back to the moment that I was sleeping under a bridge, homeless, and hungry, and feeling like no one ever loved me in this world.

The fear of loneliness kept me from living my life. The fear of rejection kept me from being who I wanted to be. The fear of abandonment kept me from speaking my mind, and defending myself.

This little 3-year-old inside of me would come to orchestrate so much of my life, I had later realized. She alone ended up dictating so much of why I had entered the marriage in the first place.

So I finally made the decision to acknowledge her but not surrender to her fears and worries, (and believe me, it was an active daily decision). I spoke to her. I held her. I loved her. And I held space for all that she needed. But I chose to walk as a woman who believed in herself, and face the unknown; to face my fears head on, and realize that *"I might very well end up alone, dying alone, never having anyone to care for me in life, but I must be willing to take a leap of faith and say that I believe my life's purpose holds greater weight than my pain, my past, and my insecurities that led me here."*

... I made a promise to myself that I would always acknowledge the pain within me, but never again be driven to action by it.

I left my marriage... and I cried... and I questioned... and I wondered... and I hated... and I begged... and I pleaded... and I acted in shame... and I screamed... and I doubted... and I blamed...

But, I finally found peace through the chaos, and redemption, and freedom.

I wrote a letter to her (which I never sent to her) called, "The Greatest Love Letter I've Never Written." The letter was an apology. It was an apology for not pushing her to be more, to do more, to see more of herself.

It was an apology for not being willing to look beyond my fears, and actively participate in acting upon every single fucking insecurity that popped up in my head. It was an apology for allowing her to do the same thing.

For not being willing to walk away years before, and realizing that we could still love each other, but we no longer needed to hurt each other. And it was a letter of me taking 100% full responsibility for what had happened to my own life, and asking for forgiveness for blaming her for where I was, and who I had become.

My ex isn't a bad person. She's a wonderful person actually. She's just not heading where I am heading, and the relationship was significant enough that I found the stagnancy, and lack of joint understanding of my new path, debilitating.

I knew that this path wasn't hers, as much as I knew she didn't belong to me, as I never did her. **Everything about our life together was nothing more than a series of actions, emotions, and decisions to mask the deeper truths within us both. We had both spent a life feeling broken, and lost, and we found familiarity within one another because of it.**

The only difference was that I was no longer willing to live in any space that felt familiar. I no longer wanted to be anywhere I had ever been before. I needed something new. Because, for me, it had come down to my willingness to discover a NEW me, or finally discarding what was left of the old me. Yes, it had truly come down to that, for me.

Perhaps we didn't spend our days fighting epic battles... but the chaos of our relationship still held 100% of the childhood hurt that never left either of our hearts. And from there we battled for comfort...

THE ACTIVE CHOICE OF DISCOMFORT

So after I walked out of my marriage, I also actively chose to walk out of the majority of my friendships as well.

I looked around my life and I took some inventory, and I realized that, as my marriage had allowed us both to be stagnant, so had most of my friendships.

Most of my friendships were "*Fans*," as I've described above. My life had been filled with people who allowed me to continue living the bullshit life I had been living thus far.

I'm not kidding when I say, I literally fired half of my employees, deleted half of my "*contact list*" on my cell phone, blocked and "*un-friended*" half of "*friends*" on Facebook, and I became quite content with the feeling of "*aloneness*" through it all.

I discovered that people take up space in our worlds. And the space that they take up is high priced real estate, that we should be very careful about sharing this space with.

The moment I got rid of my "*old friends*," suddenly new, deeper, greater, more meaningful friendships appeared, out of nowhere.

Suddenly I had attracted before me a world of people who were on the same path as me.

I began a new relationship with someone who saw me for the great work of art that I was becoming. Someone who (a year prior to me) chose to walk out of her own marriage, simply because it wasn't serving either of them, despite it being "*comfortable*" in ways. Someone who was willing to wander the earth on her own, and willing to risk it all to find truth within herself. Someone who, like me, had made many mistakes in her life, and needed to learn forgiveness, and discover epic truths by facing epic hardships.

And then I started healing... and growing... and learning... and loving... and forgiving... and finding my way back home...

But, I think it's interesting to look back in hindsight and see that what truly started the epic change within, was a willingness to jump from a ledge into seeming darkness, and being willing to give up control over it all, and walk in faith.

So I reminded myself of the first story I told you... the truth is that the greatest miracle of my life happened at a point where I had no control over anything.

Being adopted at the age of 3, from a land of prostitution, and epidemic and systemic poverty, and being placed in a space where I could become all that I am today (and still becoming) was the greatest miracle that I could never have worked out on my own if I tried.

So I closed my eyes, I took a running leap off of the edge and I jumped...

MY PERSONAL HEALING PRACTICE TO PEACE

HOW I FOUND MY WAY BACK HOME...

There are definitely some things that I have discovered that can tremendously help you get your life on track, if you're truly willing to do the work.

Whether you have come from a life of hardship and abuse as I have, or if you've just found yourself off track and taken down by a single moment of pain... I believe that I have found the remedy and path to freedom for all.

You have to remember, however, that this is the hard part. Doing the work is the part that's going to break you down, and rebuild you. Reading this book is the easy part.

Highlighting things that "speak to you" and fantasizing about change is all easy.

But truly being willing to look at yourself, and your own life, and say, I ACCEPT FULL RESPONSIBILITY FOR ALL OF IT, and I AM WILLING TO DO ANYTHING NECESSARY TO GET MY LIFE BACK ON TRACK, MY HEART HEALED, and MY SPIRIT PLUGGED BACK INTO SOURCE.

I am ready.
I am willing.
I am open.
I am going to be the freaking hero of my own story.

So, let's do this!

LET THE HEALING BEGIN...

LIFE CHANGE # 1

THE WORDS WE SPEAK BECOME THE HOUSE WE LIVE IN.

We are going to start by changing the words that come out of your mouth.

#1. No blaming. From this point forward in your life, you are no longer allowed to blame anyone for anything that has to do with you. We may discover through this process that not all things are your fault, but for now we are going to completely divorce ourselves from the "victim" mentality.

I spoke to a friend recently who I have dubbed as the "*QUEEN OF VICTIMS.*" She has a life history of relationships that all ended disastrously; from all of her siblings, to her mother, to both of her ex-husbands, to many of her friends.

And each and every single time she tells the story of "*what happened*" she is always (always) the "*victim*" in the situation.

When I pointed this out to her, and asked her how it's possible that she is truly always "*the victim*" (prompting her to consider perhaps another conclusion), she said, "*Oh, I'm not a victim, I'm a survivor of everyone's ill will towards me.*"

Aaaaand SCENE. Drop Mic. Walk off. Move on.

This is nothing more than one woman's refusal to take responsibility on a level that is epically daunting, frustrating, and shocking. My thoughts? If you're truly thinking you're always the victim... I'd consider whether or not you're actually always the perpetrator.

I know this is a harsh 180 degree reality to consider, but I think it needs to be said. And I'll venture a bet that if this describes you, chances are many people in your life have felt this way too.

I've grown up being abusive to others, taking advantage of situations and people, and lying to myself and others to deflect the truths within me that I could not accept. However, I have never considered that *"everyone in my life is wrong, and I am always right."*

This perspective is nothing more than a sad deflection of someone's inability to accept their own faults, truths, and consequences.

If you are in this space where you truly feel that you are *"always"* wronged, you're always the victim, others are always trying to hurt you, and take you down, I would urge you to seek counseling... and not with someone who allows you to cultivate this narcissistic perspective, but rather with someone who is willing to look you square in the eyes and say, *"honey....you've got some work to do here too."*

You'll never grow, you'll never be more than you are now, and you'll never find peace and freedom if you're never willing to be honest about your own culpability in things.

And, you can't do this from a *"victim/survivor"* perspective. You have to do it from a hardcore willingness to take full responsibility.

No more blaming. No more excusing your behavior and pointing fingers. No more judging the actions of others while you're all too forgiving with your own.

NO MORE. PLAYING. THE VICTIM.

In order to start healing, we absolutely must get out of the victim mentality. This mindset precludes us from truly being honest about a situation.

It's the story at the beginning of this book about the husband who cheated on his wife and left, and her complete refusal to be honest about what drove her husband to cheat and ultimately feel that he needed distance and a fresh start from their entire family.

Had she been honest with their kids and with herself all along and said, "*My actions caused your father to feel as though he needed some space so that he could heal. Don't blame him anymore than you do me. It is our responsibility now to carry him through this, and love him the most,*" the relationship between her and her ex and their children would be so much more positive.

But she can't handle that her initial action of knocking down that first domino caused a full ocean of distance between the father and children. It was too much to bear. So she became a victim and she lied to all around her to mask her own pain.

The lies we tell the world around us are nothing more than a defense mechanism to hide the pain within us.

It's okay to forgive yourself for this. It's understandable. No one will fault you for lying... but once you admit and can learn from this, you must move forward into a different, more positive space.

No more being a victim. No more lying, or using "*alternative facts*" to mask the painful truth.

#2. No more sad, pathetic, depressed "speech." We're going to stop using depressing language to describe ourselves and our lives. We are also going to stop referring to ourselves as *"broken," "depressed," "sad," "messed up,"* or whatever negative title you've spoken over your life. STOP.

From this moment forward you are not allowed to ever say those things again. I wrote down all of the ways that I wanted someone to describe me... and I used that description to start describing myself.

I literally thought, *"How would I want to someone to describe me if they were introducing me, or asking someone else if they knew me?"*

Here is what I wrote:

"Kristy Sinsara is an amazingly successful business owner. Everything she touches turns to gold, as she has truly discovered the secret to building success from the ashes of ruin. She is wildly engaging, entertaining, and intelligent; and she has become a best-selling author with a number one blog. She is a true inspiration to millions who follow her."

I literally wrote that when I was depressed and quasi-suicidal. Do you know how true this is for me now? Every single word of this has come to pass, just a few short years later.

WRITE DOWN HOW YOU WANT TO BE DESCRIBED TO OTHERS OR INTRODUCED IN LIFE. And don't leave out a single detail...

LIFE CHANGE # 2

INTENTIONAL LIVING

In the same way that you have probably never just got into your car without any clue where you're going, you shouldn't do this in life. Don't just drive around aimlessly. Trust me, you'll run out of gas before you know it (if you haven't already).

You must start living with **INTENTION**. You must wake up daily with a specific purpose. You must start working towards goals. You must **STOP** living on autopilot. And you must stop living purposelessly.

> **MOST PEOPLE NEVER ATTAIN THEIR PRIMARY GOALS BECAUSE THEY ARE CONSTANTLY SIDETRACKED BY SECONDARY ACTIVITIES.**
>
> **– LES BROWN**

Intentional living is everything.

What do you want your life to look like? **WHAT DO YOU TRULY WANT YOUR LIFE TO LOOK LIKE?** Don't just write a book and hope it sells. Imagine yourself on a stage being introduced in front of thousands of people who have already read your book, and relate to it, and love you for it.

Don't just get through some college degree and "*hope*" for a job. Imagine yourself IN that career. What are you doing? How happy are you? How fulfilled are you?

One of my very best friends in life, Laurie Hudson, decided at the age of 36 that she was going to go to college and receive her nursing degree. At the age of 40 she graduated from college with her Bachelor of Science in Nursing. And the whole time she was in school she was saying, *"I'm going to be the Manager of the largest Level 1 Trauma Center in my state within 10 years."* She didn't just have a goal to graduate, but a goal to BE someone afterwards; and not just *"someone,"* someone **specific**. She attained this goal within six short years.

Since then, she has surpassed every single goal she has created for herself. And these are goals that most would think were impossible to attain, with her level of experience or practice. However, she continues to set goals and she continues to knock each goal straight out of the park, each and every time.

She is now going for her Masters of Science in Nursing with a focus on Leadership and Management.

So, what makes Laurie more successful than so many of her colleagues? What makes her able to effectuate her goals seemingly more than others? Does she have some magical pixy fairy dust that she blows into the Universe as she makes a wish? NOPE. She has but one single sword by her side, and it is the sword of self-awareness driven by faith. She knows that she knows that she knows that she can.... and so she does, with all of the intention of the Universe behind her.

She directs her goals into action by a simple step-by-step process.

Truly my friends, **THE WHOLE UNVERSE IS CONSPIRING FOR YOU**.... as it has and always will for Laurie. You are no different.

Laurie was willing to believe in something greater than she had ever known before. This practice in itself is an action of extreme discipline all in itself. This isn't always easy to do, and often requires daily mindfulness, and focus.

She was also willing to work towards something in faith, without any evidence that it was guaranteed ahead of her.

It's like as if the pavement didn't show up until you take the step, and put your foot down, and suddenly it appears before you, to hold you, and support you. This is faith. Faith isn't knowing for sure the pavement is there to catch you; faith is the belief in things unseen.

The greater the faith, the greater the reward.
The greater your ability to walk towards things with the absolute knowledge that it is all yours for the taking, the greater your treasure will be.

Faith doesn't need your knowledge of the future, and it certainly doesn't need your control.

The more you plan and plot, and do everything possible to make sure you absolutely cannot fail, the more you're not acting in faith.

THE POWER OF A DREAM BOARD

I want you to go to the store, buy two poster boards, get out some fun creative markers, and spend at least a solid hour creating a **DREAM/ INTENTION/GRATITUDE BOARD.**

On the first board is going to be nothing but words that we want to manifest in your life. Hope. Love. Kindness. Abundance. Friendships. Love. Career. Wholeness. Peace. ETC.

Next, (in between all of those words) I want you to write down all of the things that you want to be known for in this life. Great mom. Amazing partner. Dynamic Speaker. Best-Selling Author. Intelligent. Fun. Wild. Adventurous. ER Nurse Director. Most successful car salesman. Most sought-after dentist in your town.

Be specific about it all, leaving out no single detail... And from the point when you've finished this board forward, you are no longer allowed to refer to yourself as anything other than the things that are on this board.

LIFE CHANGE # 3

MANIFESTING YOUR DESIRES THROUGH MEDITATION

People call me the *"QUEEN OF MANIFESTIONS."* I have created an uncanny ability to manifest anything that I desire before me. People have literally introduced me as such (and it's a wildly powerful reality to hold true).

So how did I get this amazing title? How did I get to a point of being able to manifest things so quickly before me?

One simple reality I discovered. A fantasy is stronger than reality, therefore making our emotions more effective than our thoughts. I learned the art of manifesting the **FEELING, NOT** the "**thing.**"

I don't just say, *"I want to be a best-selling author."* I imagine what it feels like to be standing on a stage with thousands (literally) of people in front of me, most of whom have already read my books and can relate to me and feel a connection with me, and love and adore and support me. I soak up that feeling, I breathe it in, and I give thanks out loud for it.

I breathe in the abundance of love around me, I accept it, and I offer gratitude for it.

And I open my eyes while standing on that stage, and the crowd in front of me is clapping and laughing. And they are yelling *"THANK YOU"* and *"we love you"* and *"you helped me find my own way"* and *"because of your willingness to be so vulnerable in your latest book, I have found my own path."*

And I yell *"THANK YOUUUUUUU..."* to myself, and to the Universe, and to the crowd, for the abundance of purpose that is coursing through my veins in this moment.

And the very next day I get a call asking if I'd like to be the keynote speaker at one of the largest women's business conference's on the West Coast. Why? Because one of the presenters has read my book and feels that I can be a great asset to the stage for the women present.

30 DAYS OF MANIFESTATION

EVERY SINGLE DAY for 30 solid days, you must wake up, look at this board, and spend (at least) 5 minutes meditating on what it feels like to be living this life in your future.

Be specific. I'm going to keep repeating the importance of this over, and over, and over.

Sit there and truly soak this in, feel the feeling moving through you. The excitement. The greatness. The hope. The happiness. The smiles. The laughter. The abundance. **FEEL IT...**

Remember, the trick to manifesting anything before you is not to imagine the "*thing*," it's to imagine the "*feeling*" associated with that thing. Don't just imagine you're in a new career. Imagine what it feels like to be you in that new career. What does it feel like to be sitting at that desk? Or driving that car? How do you feel in your new home, etc?

LIFE CHANGE # 4

GRATITUDE

It is a true statement to say *"Those who say thank you will always have the most to say thank you for."*

Gratitude begets abundance. Gratitude is the doorway to all that you desire. It is imperative that you begin to understand the importance of this. Say *"THANK YOU"* **ALWAYS... FOR LITERALLY EVERYTHING.**

If you're sitting there having some sad, pathetic moment feeling like your life sucks and there's no purpose in it, I want you to consider the reality of what would happen if what you did have was taken from you? Perhaps you don't have a nice car, but you have A car? Perhaps you don't have a car at all, but you live next to a bus station. Perhaps you don't live next to a bus station but you at least have a job to walk to.

The truth is that if there is anything in your life that you would not want taken from you, then you have something to be grateful for.

When I was acting pitiful and playing the *"victim"* role, I would say I *"had nothing."* But when I considered what would happen if I didn't even have what I had... I made a list.

Maybe I wasn't where I wanted to be, but I certainly wasn't as low as I could be. So I focused on gratitude for all that was around me.

I got to a point where I was literally driving through green lights and just laughing out loud, saying, *"Thank you,"* as if that green light was there just for me.

Eventually the surface of you becomes the depth of you, and before you know it you aren't *"acting"* grateful, you wake up one day and you **ARE GRATEFUL.**

You become the embodiment of gratitude itself. You become the personification of pure thankfulness. And, this single act of honest joy begets abundance... and other epic things...

GRATITUDE IS THE GATEWAY

TO ABUNDANCE

Never stop saying "*thank you.*" Never stop feeling thankful. Nothing is ever too small to offer gratitude.

WHAT CAN YOU SAY THANK YOU FOR TO THOSE WHO HAVE CAUSED YOU GREAT PAIN?

I feel like it's important to understand that my mom was NOT a bad mom. She was a wonderful example of many things that I witnessed, and later emulated in life.

The truth is that the only reason my dad had so many opportunities to try and sexually assault me was because my mom was constantly at work, essentially supporting a family of five all on her own.

She had taken a career, without any prior education and only on-the-job training, and ended up working for one of the most renowned Dermatologists in Oklahoma City, and was working essentially as a Physicians Assistant for the majority of my life.

She was extremely dedicated to her profession, and very good at her art. She was dedicated to keeping a family together, as dysfunctional as it may have been. You could tell that her one single motivating factor was "*normalcy.*"

She came from a broken home of her own, and I think she was over-motivated by "*tradition*" because of this.

But truth be told, I love the tradition she implemented in my life. I never missed a birthday, a Christmas, a holiday, a hot meal on the table, a refrigerator full of groceries, or a chance to be a kid, in any other way offered.

I was given the opportunity to play any sport, try and any instrument, take any lesson, do anything I wanted, essentially because of her hard work.

Yes, I resented her for not being the kind of mom to me that I witnessed she had chosen to be to my sister, but I also appreciated the mom that she was.

This is why the betrayal ran so much deeper with her. I could see that she made decisions to love, or not love, to hug or not hug, to spend time with or not, otherwise, with each of us. I was never high on her priority list, which seemed to consist only of *"bringing home the bacon"*, *"frying it up in the pan,"* and making sure my sister had all that she needed to be successful otherwise.

And her decisions fed straight into this continued narrative that I was not good enough for anyone... not a dad to love me, or a mom to care about me.

But part of my healing process was taking a step out of my own situation, and experience, and seeing her, not as a daughter, but as another spiritual being, with her own set of life lessons, and issues she was dealing with all on her own.

LIFE CHANGE # 5

STOP PERSONALIZING WHAT HURT YOU

This is going to sound crazy, but do you know one of the greatest things that happened to me as a little girl, which helped me get through my childhood? It was the time my dad came to me and told me he could no longer try to make love to me (irrespective of his perception of our mutual desire for this). I was 9 years old when he said this to me.

What I realized in that moment was that my dad was bat shit fucking crazy. I realized instantly that his craziness didn't actually have anything to do with me. The dude was just fucking nuts. Like seriously fucking nuts.

The truth is that people just shoot their arrows in life.

Those arrows can be arrows of *"crazy," "selfish," "depressed," "refusal to take responsibility," "anger,"* etc. But the most important thing to know about the arrows that people point and shoot at you is that they have nothing to do with you. They're not actually pointing "at" you, they're just pointing... and you just so happen to be in their line of fire.

The truth is that whether you were there or not, that arrow would have gotten shot, and it would have hit someone.

Stop acting like you're some dirty cop who is trying to entrap people. Stop taking responsibility for the downfalls of those around you. It's not your fault that your dad tried to rape you. It has nothing to do with you.

I have a friend who was raped in college and she played out the event of her rape over and over and over for years. She couldn't stop wondering what would have happened had she just "*not*" taken that path back to her dorm alone. She beat herself up for drinking too much. She hated herself for putting herself in the position of being able to be raped.

I remember saying to her, "*You sound crazy when you take responsibility for being raped. You sound like a fucking lunatic actually. As if it was entrapment of your rapist. As if to say, if you weren't there, and someone else was, he wouldn't have done it to her. Is that what you mean? Do you honestly believe that had any other woman taken that dark path home, alone and quasi drunk, she would not have been a victim of this man?*"

It's like she's saying this guy is a nice and reputable guy otherwise, but because she decided to drink a little too much, and take a dark path home, this really outstanding human being ended up doing something really awful to her. She took the blame for both of us.

Listen up, **ALL WHO HAVE BEEN SEXUALLY ABUSED**: Don't be as crazy as your perpetrator, and don't let them take the best part of you away. They definitely don't deserve that level of power over you.

If you want to get back at your perpetrator, then be stronger for it. Be more compassionate because of it. Be more of a leader and someone who inspires others through it. Don't hide away in the shadows of shame because of something that happened. NO matter how "*big*" that something was.

YOU ARE BIGGER THAN IT.

You're stronger than anything that's ever happened to you.

LIFE CHANGE # 6

FORGIVENESS AND COMPASSION

There is literally nothing more important than this single step. I should have started with it, but the truth is that you must come to this realization through processing everything before it. You can't start here, because **HERE** is a daunting and difficult space to be in, if you begin here. But if you've done the work up to now, forgiveness is easier than you'll realize.

You cannot move forward in your life until you're prepared to forgive yourself, and all and any who you perceive to have hurt you.

I wrote a letter to myself and I said, "*I'm sorry.*"
"*I'm sorry that I let people abuse you, Kristy, and I'm sorry that I turned around and abused you more.*"

You cannot move into a space of wholeness without forgiving everything and everyone. Yes, everyone.

ACCEPT RESPONSIBILITY FOR WHAT HAS HURT YOU THE MOST and FORGIVE YOURSELF.

I knew a woman who told me her mother had forced her to have an abortion when she was 16 years old. She said that she's tried and tried to forgive her mom, but she just can't.

And so I suggested that it's not her mom that needs forgiveness, but perhaps her. She needs to get to a point of forgiving herself.

And when I suggested this she literally flipped out on me and yelled, "*It wasn't my fault, it wasn't my fault. She made me.*"

The truth is that I don't know if it's true that this woman's mom forced her to have an abortion. But I do know that, irrespective of who is to blame, there is self-forgiveness that needs to happen within her heart. It doesn't matter whether it was ultimately her fault. She clearly still needs to forgive herself for it in the end.

So I suggested perhaps she forgive herself for not being strong enough to stand up to her mom at the time. And she broke down into tears and fell to her knees, and she said, "*No... it was my fault. I did this. I did this. I did this. And I just want to die. I deserve to die along with my baby.*"

NO. You don't deserve to die. You deserve to live. But right now you're not doing either. You're stuck in the in-between barely alive, wishing for death upon you.

You deserve to forgive yourself, and you deserve to live.

I, too, remember being a pregnant teenager, flippantly thinking, "*Maybe I'll sell my baby to some rich couple and take the money and travel the world.*"

Oh God, the thought of it embarrasses me and shames me. How young and naïve I was. I didn't know how it felt to give birth to a child when I had those thoughts. I didn't' know how it felt to hold your own baby in your arms when I contemplated this reality. I didn't know... and I beat myself up just for thinking it, over and over. So I learned to forgive myself for not knowing what I didn't know when I didn't know it.

> **FORGIVE YOURSELF FOR NOT KNOWING**
> **WHAT YOU DIDN'T KNOW WHEN YOU DIDN'T KNOW IT.**

It's okay. It's all a part of the process and molding of becoming you. It's all a part of the process of you getting to the point where you're reading this book, and hearing these words, and applying these actions for change.

FORGIVE YOURSELF.

Believe me when I say it is YOU that YOU are seeking the most forgiveness in this lifetime from!

FORGIVE THEM ALL.

Next, you must forgive all actions against you. The actions against you which were never personal to you, had nothing to do with you, and they were a part of someone else's path.

I consider this single idea that IF we did call forth this life and all of the lessons in it, I would certainly choose over and over and over again to be the victim instead of the perpetrator in my own play.

I am glad I came into this life as "*me*" and not my father. I can handle being the kid who was sexually abused more than I could handle being the man who tried to rape a child of her innocence. For what? For an orgasm? For a moment of control? The reality of what my father had to live with is a far greater burden to bear, if I'm being honest.

Can you be honest about the perpetrators in your own life and say the same thing? Before my father died, he gave me the opportunity to tell him that I had forgiven him.

But to be really honest with you, I didn't let him know that I forgave him out of an act of kindness. I let him know I forgave him out of one single last act of defiance, to let him know that NOT EVEN HIS ABUSE could control me! "*I forgive you*" was my way of saying, "*You no longer have dominion over me.*" As if he were some demon living inside of me; I stood my ground, and claimed my space, and I exorcised him from within! (Amen).

I told him I forgave him long before I had actually forgiven him because it was my way of cutting the cord between us, and letting him know (definitively) that he no longer had control over me. The power of the words, "*I forgive you*" is mighty!

SAYING "*I FORGIVE YOU*" is a powerful step towards ACTUAL forgiveness. You don't need to be there yet in order to say it. It can simply be the first step on a long journey ahead.

And it wasn't until I said those words, that I actually began the process of forgiving him, and took that first step.

THE IMPORTANCE OF A RITUAL OF FORGIVENESS

A great way to begin the process of forgiveness is by memorializing it somehow. I personally wrote a letter to myself, forgiving myself; and then I wrote a letter to my father forgiving him.

Then I took those letters and I merged them together in a fire ceremony. I took several rocks and wrote the words "*Gratitude*," "*Peace*," "*Compassion*," "*Wholeness*," and "*Love*" on them, buried the ashes of the letter, and placed the rocks over the burial space.

I know others who have written words on stones and thrown them into the ocean. I know others who have had actual cord-cutting ceremonies with healers.

A very good friend of mine, Julia Junkin, is a Sufi Healer. She performs "Cord Cuttings" to untether your soul from a thing, an event, a person, or a situation, so that you can be free to move forward.

I think this is an epically powerful way to move forward past the trauma of accepting responsibility for things we have otherwise refused to acknowledge.

WHAT IS YOUR RITUAL?

Whatever feels right to you, do that. But I would strongly encourage you to do something that symbolizes this step to freedom. Memorialize this epic event so that you always have something to remember this moment by.

This way, if you ever feel yourself digressing, you can turn to this memory and say, "*Nope, I've already forgiven myself. I'm not going to sit here and participate in guilt or self-hate or self-destruction.*"

Had Chicken Man sought a healing counselor, he could have learned to accept the reality that it wasn't his fault that his family died in that fire. Like I said earlier, we are going to realize through the process of self-forgiveness that not everything is our fault. It's imperative that we aren't "*blamers*," and "*deflectors*" but it's equally important that we aren't walking around with pain that doesn't belong to us, or unwarranted.

He could have come to terms with his spontaneous decision to jump out of a window without considering the ramifications, understanding that it was a decision not based in cognitive reasoning but a natural human reaction to survival. He has been programmed to jump out of a window during a fire. It wasn't his fault.

He could have learned to stop beating himself up and punishing himself over and over and over. And he could have taken the pictures of his loved ones and asked for forgiveness, accepted responsibility, and (above all things) allowed them to not die in vain by making it his life purpose to teach the act of forgiveness from a perspective that would have captivated the world over.

Forgiveness must come with compassion. Be good to yourself. Be kinder to yourself than you ever have before. Hold yourself when you cry. Talk to yourself out loud. Spend time with yourself more.

THE PURPOSE IN YOUR PAIN

The next step in the healing process is to allow this to change you in the way that it's supposed to change you.

Allow it to recreate you, and mold you in a way that you begin to visibly take new form. Be changed so drastically that you can look back and feel like that person is no longer who you are today. Be unrecognizable.

People that knew me several years ago will tell you that I don't even seem like the same person anymore. This is the greatest compliment and testimony to my healing process.

I don't seem like the same person because I am not the same person. Kristy Sinsara was reborn, restructured, and recreated out of the ashes of responsibility. The old me no longer exists. She's a part of my past.

LIFE CHANGE # 7

FAITH AND HOPE

I have always said that if hope were a grain of sand represented on all of the beaches in all of the world, I had come down to having one single small grain left within me.

After my brother died, I broke into a million pieces and I could not pick myself up off the floor. It's like suddenly in the moment he left me in this life my entire life flashed back before me, but it only showed the parts where I fucked it all up.

It showed the time my brother begged me to go to lunch with him and I reluctantly agreed, and sat on my cell phone the entire time while he was trying to connect with me. Had I known that would be the last lunch I would ever eat with him I would have put my fucking phone down.

It showed me the time that I got pregnant and couldn't take care of my own child and was sleeping underneath a bridge, begging the devil to take my life because it was obvious God no longer loved me enough to do it. It showed me the time that I had stolen something from some stupid store and got arrested and had a record that would follow me for the rest of my life. For what? A moment of attention? Well, I certainly have received what I asked for with this one.

It showed me every broken moment, every lost decision, and every horrible mistake I had ever made. And I couldn't take it anymore. I couldn't take this life anymore. I couldn't stop seeing my brother's face, standing across the parking lot yelling, "*I LOVE YOU SIS*," and me rolling my eyes and walking back into my office.

I kept begging God for a chance to take it all back, do it all over, just one more chance to talk to him.

Had I known that would be the last time I heard him yell those words at me, as he did our entire life long, I would have stopped in that moment and ran over to him, and put my arms around his neck, and looked into his eyes and said, *"You loving me is one of the only things that has ever kept me alive. THANK YOU. I love you too. Thank you for being such an amazing brother."*

I could not come to terms with who I had become. What I had done with my life.

YOU HAVE TO BELIEVE IN SOMETHING MORE.

None of this holds purpose unless you're willing to believe for something more. **YOU MUST** believe in something more, something greater than yourself, and something ahead of you.

You have to believe in your purpose in this life. There is **ONLY ONE YOU ON THIS PLANET.** This is an undeniable truth. Even if you're a twin, there's still only **ONE YOU.**

Your life holds purpose on this planet, as does everyone's. You are a great part of the balance of humanity. I personally believe that it is our individual imbalance that has tipped the scale of humanity off kilter. If everyone on this planet was living their divine purpose and power, there would be no wars, no sadness, no global epidemic of hunger. There would only be us, individually, living as one.

WHAT DO YOU HAVE TO BRING TO THIS TABLE?

There is something within you that you must bring forth in a way that no one else has, or can. There is something screaming to come out of you... some idea you're pregnant with, a thought wanting to birth a book, an action ready to birth a movement. SOMETHING IS THERE. Follow your passions within you, and they will lead you to great discoveries of your life, and your purpose, and your path!

LIFE CHANGE # 8

START ON THE OUTSIDE

It seems contradictory to say this, to start outside of yourself, but one of the best things that I did for myself was when I started volunteering my time to help others.

There's something that happens to us when we help others. It is one of the most healing things you can do actually. I got outside of my own head, and I focused on helping someone other than myself.

This was wildly therapeutic. We all become the medicine we need the most in life. We become the therapy we need to hear. When we are truly ready for growth, we learn to give others what we need to give ourselves, and through this process we begin to transform.

I started helping others who were depressed. I started posting positive quotes, and thoughts, and lessons I had learned, online. And people started following me.

When was the last time you did anything for anyone but yourself or your own tribe? When was the last time you offered someone an anonymous gift? When was the last time you shared your time, and gave someone hope, or help?

I made a list called, "*30 Days of Kindness,*" and I stuck to that list for 30 solid days. Every single day I did something for someone that wasn't me.

I left my favorite book in a park with a note to whoever found it about how it changed my life and what it meant to me to read it. I wrote a "*thank you*" letter to someone who had helped me along the way that I hadn't yet truly offered gratitude for yet. I placed a penny in a parking lot, heads up, just so someone could find it and feel "*lucky.*" I bought two homeless people lunch at a nearby restaurant. I made 25 sack lunches and took them to the bus station. I did these things for 30 days in a row, and I kicked off my "*new me*" with kindness and compassion for others.

Make a list of 30 days of kindness and compassion of your own, and stick to it. In fact, you should start NOTHING in life without doing this first.

LIFE CHANGE #9

THE PERSON WHO HURT YOU CAN'T HEAL YOU

This is about moving forward, not backward. This is about walking in new spaces you have never walked in before, and finding new meadows unscathed by your own pain and experience.

> The answer to your pain is not in your past.
> It is in the pain itself!

This is an epic part of the healing process – to truly understand this truth. Most people feel hurt by a specific person, and they run back to that person to try and help them work through the pain. As if the person can suddenly erase what has been said or done, as if they have a magic ability to heal a scar just because they've created it.

It's like asking the pavement to erase the pain after you've just plowed into it on your bike. The pavement has nothing to do with the healing process. It was there to teach you a lesson, not to reconcile your wounds.

I truly do believe that this is one of the reasons why so many abused kids find their way into abusive relationships. Because they are trying to go back to a familiar space and rewrite the past. They are trying to go back to a place they recognize and see if they can fix it. As if revisiting a specific scenario will help them resolve their pain.

I grew up being abused, and then I actively participated in seeking out abusive relationships without realizing what I was doing.

The more "*normal*" the person was, the less interested I was in cultivating a relationship with them. YES there was a truth of familiarity that drew me to them. I had been conditioned to believe that this was "*normal*" in my own way, or acceptable.

But I was also drawn to them because I was on a mission to discover something within myself... I just couldn't figure out what (or how or why). And the only people I believed who could provide me with any understanding was the people who most resembled the ones who hurt me the most.

I sought out abusive relationships to try to heal the pain within me. It was my way of going back to the abuser to heal the pain.

Moving forward is the answer to healing, not backward. It's not necessary to physically revisit the past when we are trying to move into the future.

LIFE CHANGE #10

GIVE BACK

IF YOU KNOW – TEACH
Another part of the healing process is to give back to the world the energy of your new wholeness and truth.

This is an important step because it is where you exchange the energy of pain and sadness that you once created with the energy of love, truth, enlightenment, and hope for others.

Help push others forward. Submit your will to the Spirit and give to the collective consciousness of humanity by being a guiding light for others behind you.

OFFER GRATITUDE FOR YOUR PAIN, FOR IT IS THE GATEWAY TO YOUR SOUL.

If I started with this at step one you wouldn't have even bothered reading this book. It is insane to consider offering gratitude for our painful journeys that bring us to our knees.

Yet once you have truly discovered wholeness and healing, and have come full circle with all of this, your final step is to offer gratitude.

In the beginning of this process, gratitude is the most difficult thing to consider; yet by the end it is the easiest part of all.

If you've truly healed, grown, and moved forward, you will freely and willingly offer gratitude for the journey behind you and gratefully move forward into a new awareness of your truths.

PART 5.

LOVE LETTERS TO MYSELF

HEALING LETTERS TO MY INNER CHILD

One of the most healing things that I have ever done, as instructed by my persona.

I spiritual guru, Jane Hiatt, was to write letters to myself at every age that I had felt "**broken**."

This was one of the most difficult things I have ever done. It was actually difficult to even begin to "*acknowledge*" the child within me who was hurting still from the pain of my past. I was one of those who always believed that as long as I didn't acknowledge it, it didn't really happen.

The problem being that every single time you go through something traumatic, it's almost as if the child within you (at the age of however old you were at the time) stays right there in that moment. And they will scream at you through the rest of your life. They will remind you at all costs that they are still there. They will never let you forget about them.

Jane encouraged me to allow her to hypnotize me and allow her to see who all was still in there, hurting.

Of course, 3 year old Kristy... standing on that chair in an orphanage in Thailand, looking out the window... feeling so alone in this world, wondering why she is all alone?

The 9 year-old girl, whose father attempted to rape her, still scared out of her fucking mind.

The 11 year-old girl whose mom told her to take off her panties so her father could beat her with a belt, while he got sexually turned on.

The 15 year-old who allowed someone she barely knew to take away her virginity, thinking that as long as she was in control of giving it up that no one else would try to steal it from her.

The 40 year-old woman who heard her mom make fun of her for being "*defiant*" as a teenager, as if to dismiss all reasons for the behavior.

It is imperative that you do this exercise!

It is SO imperative actually that I'm going to share with you the my very personal letters I wrote to my younger "*selves.*"

The hurting children within you must be acknowledged.
They must be understood, and loved.
They must be healed.
And they must be set free.

DEAR 3 YEAR-OLD KRISTY:

Oh man little girl. How scared are you right now? God... who wouldn't be? Shit!

I see you standing there on that chair in that orphanage, looking out the window, wondering if your mom will ever come back for you. Feeling so scared right now, So alone in the world. Wondering what you did wrong?

You didn't do anything wrong. You don't know this yet but you have grand purpose in this life, and that purpose calls for you to live very far away from here. It mandates that you be taken in this moment, and feel this deep seeded aloneness that you feel.

This feeling of abandonment within you, actually ends up creating an incredible sense of independence within you later. The truth is that because of your ability to be here in this moment, we actually become quite amazing, you and I, together!

I just want to hold you so tight, and tell you that it's all going to be okay. I want to kiss your adorable little cheeks and squeeze you so tight.

I promise it all ends great.... but THIS moment, right here... this is the true beginning of the rest of our lives. This is the true beginning of the making of a life NINJA! I love you.

DEAR 9 YEAR-OLD KRISTY:

OMG HONEY. HOLY SHIT. I am sorry. I am SO sorry that you had to deal with that asshole. You have to come curl up on my lap and let me hold you. My heart literally beats 100 mph for you as I even type this, thinking of you. You are so scared. You're so angry. So confused. The world is no longer as you once thought. I get that. I just want to run my fingers through your hair, and wipe away your tears, and place my hand over your beating heart and tell you how much I love you.

I wish I could go back in time and take you out of this situation. I can see you standing there, so overwhelmed with confusion, eyes wide open. I want you to know that I acknowledge the feelings you're feeling. The fear. The fact that the word "fear" doesn't describe the fear you feel. But I want you to know that it's going to be okay. I have you. I hear you. I see you. And I got this.

The greatest thing I can tell you right now is that I lived enough of our life to know that we become stronger than this man. We become stronger than him in every way. And eventually you realize this, and your strength scares him to death. You create an inner strength within you so deep and so wide, that the world wonders where this level of super heroic power comes from.

It comes from this moment... You were so brave to yell, and to not allow him to violate you anymore than he did. You later realize how brave this was, although I know right now you're feeling anything but brave. But omg baby girl, this was so incredibly brave of you what you did. YOU saved us from being truly violated.

You literally saved my life little girl. I am so proud of you. I am SO grateful for you. I'm going to hold you every single day, and love you, and tell you how grateful I am and proud of you I am until you finally get it. You are a super hero. You're MY super hero actually!

DEAR 15 YEAR-OLD KRISTY:

Part of me wants to yell at you! OMG. You fucking idiot! What in the hell were you thinking? But I know what you were thinking. You found self-worth through people wanting you. Fucking classic "sexual abuse" mentality. Jesus. You're a fucking cliché.

But I know that yelling at you, and ridiculing you, and judging you, would make me no better than our mom. I must be better to you than anyone. I must treat you with respect and love, and understanding in ways that no one else has.

So I'm going to take a deep breath and I'm going to hold you first and tell you that I forgive you and I love you, and I am sorry too.

I know the truth is that this wasn't an "accidental" act of immaturity. It actually was a deliberate act of sadness, loneliness and desperation that got you pregnant. You grew up feeling like you never belonged to anyone or anything, and this was your way of being tethered to someone, something outside of yourself.

I remember your first memory when you realized you were pregnant... you fantasized about taking your son (yes you knew from second ONE that it was a boy), to McDonald's and watching him eat a burger, and you sitting there thinking of how much you loved him. Jesus. You don't even fucking eat McDonald's. LOL

Let me start with, I definitely understand WHY.

But babe, I won't sugarcoat this.... this was an epically difficult one to overcome for us... but we do it.

We attempt suicide. We find ourselves in many lost relationships. We wander the earth looking for love. We try everything possible to cover the pain. This is one of those things that we go through that changes us forever. BUT WE DO IT. And I have to tell you, with a smile on my face as I type this out, the ending of this story.

It all becomes okay in the end. Our son finds his way back to us, and we become extremely close. We find our family we were searching for all along. We have our home. We discovered our peace. He's a beautiful boy that turned into an incredible young man, full of life, as we were, full of hope, as we are, and full of potential, as we created within him. He's truly just perfect.

So if I can say any one single thing to you, it is THANK YOU.

Your sadness brought us to a level of pain we had never experienced, but the healing brought us to a level of hope we had never known existed. Thank you for being brave enough to put him up for adoption, and not abort him, as so many had suggested. Babe, you took the extremely difficult route, and you come out ahead in the end, with this amazing man by your side.

DEAR 40 YEAR-OLD KRISTY:

I know you are feeling defeated right now. No one sets out to get divorced. But if you would be truly honest with yourself you would admit that you knew this was a conclusion to this relationship that you anticipated. I hate to say, "I told you so," but... well, I AM you, so... it's pointless.

You entered this marriage for reasons that you knew were not sustainable. You wanted a family because you thought it would fill the void within you. You thought it would take away the loneliness within you. Yet, it was just another way to avoid the truth within you. But it turned out to be another seeming mistake that could have led you down a dark path.

But here's the thing, Kristy. I smile as I write this to you... This divorce ended up finally being the thing that changed us. I'm not mad at you. I love you actually for this. We finally found the thing that brought us to our knees. And do you know why this was it, out of all things before this? Because it was a decision you made NOT out of chaos, but out of truth. It was a decision that wasn't forced from confusion, but a quiet honest reflection within you that you finally listened to! Everything in your life that has created change was forced by you through some insanely chaotic situation you had gotten yourself into. But this is the first decision you've ever made out of hope, and truth, and peace, and strength.

A marriage ending, that had no real reason to end, other than your willingness to admit that your life was not on the right track. There was more for you out there. And you grew out of the relationships around you, and stayed confidently focused on what you believed could be a future that was birthed from a new awareness of who you are, and who you truly believed you could become.

And... as Elizabeth Gilbert suggests, you were willing to abandon all that you knew to find truth. You did it. You actually finally did it.

PART 6.

HEALING THROUGH RELATIONSHIPS

YOU FIRST.

In order to heal some of the relationships in your life, you may need to step away from them for a period of time. Giving yourself some space to seek truth and truly discover what you want from that relationship (if anything at all anymore) is important.

At this point in the game, the primary focus should be self-preservation, finding truth, healing, and growth. You can't focus on personal growth if you're knee deep in a relationship that's actually unhealthy.

It's much like what they say while traveling on an airplane. It's imperative that you put your own oxygen mask on first before assisting others. Why? Because you're no good if you're dead. You're also no good if you can barely breathe or if you're drowning in any capacity of your own.

It's not an act of selflessness to help people beyond your capability. It's an act of fear; and usually one that is motivated by guilt. It is imperative that you stop and take care of yourself first.

First things first, let's take some inventory of your relationships. Who is in your life now? Who is closest to you? Are these all healthy relationships? Do they all posses the mandatory elements necessary for sustainability and growth?

5 MANDATORY BASIC NEEDS THAT MUST BE MET IN ALL HEALTHY RELATIONSHIPS

1 Mutual Respect

2 Mutual Consideration

3 Mutual Trust

4 Mutual Commitment

5 Mutual Love or Understanding

This is not a smorgasbord. You are not allowed to choose your top three and discard the rest. You are not allowed to make excuses for why only 2 of the 5 exist in your marriage, and then pretend it's a *"healthy relationship."*

All 5 of these things must be present in order for any relationship – friendship, work relationship, romantic relationship – doesn't matter, to be sustainable.

Evaluate your closest relationships right now, and determine whether or not they hold all 5 basic needs.

REMOVING THE TITLES FROM OUR LIVES

One of the most healing things I have ever done is start here with all of the relationships in my life. There is literally nothing more powerful that you could ever do to remove a "*hold*" someone may have over you than by removing the title they hold over your life.

Titles come with a level of expectation, understanding, and, yes, power! Mom, dad, brother, life-long-friend, closest companion, girlfriend, husband; all of these titles come with an understanding of the built-in expectation of the relationship itself.

The biggest problem with the titles you give people is that it creates a space for abuse that you otherwise would never put up with.

I cannot tell you how many times I have heard someone say, "*Well, if she wasn't my mom, I would never deal with this.*" I say I don't give a shit if she is your mom. There is still a foundation of respect, mutual consideration, trust, and love that must be present in all sustainable relationships.

I think you should actually remove the titles from every single human being in your life right now, and then take the relationships at face value.

Whose behavior have you been excusing? Who isn't "*showing up*" for you when you need them? Which relationships feel very one-sided? How many relationships do you make excuses for because of a simple title?

Consider them all in detail.

Which ones now deserve to stay? Which ones hold the five basic needs of sustainability: Respect, Mutual Consideration, Commitment, Trust, and Love?

Any of them that do not carry all five of these aspects should be discarded. And if they cannot be wholly discarded, they should be continued only with extreme, strict boundaries that you have created.

You must remain in control of a relationship that is not serving you. Otherwise, it is going to break you down and hurt you in the end.

THREE MAIN RELATIONSHIP RULES
YOU MUST UNDERSTAND

RULE #1

All relationships outside of us merely reflect the relationship within us.

Often times, if we are the type of people who truly "*grow*" through life, we will find ourselves going from relationship to relationship, each feeling like we've "*never had this level of a connection or greatness with another human being.*" However, all this is simply a reflection of our own personal development and willingness to find ourselves on a much deeper level; each relationship reflecting the deep personal growth we have come to know within.

So, if you've been lying to yourself about what you've done, who you've been, certain "*truths*" about your past, or otherwise not being wholly present and vulnerable, this is what you can expect from those around you.

No one can truly know you more, or more deeply, or more honestly than you've been willing to know yourself. If you're shallow with yourself and your own internal thoughts...this is what will be drawn to you (others who are equally shallow); and this is the level of relationships that you will attract.

I really want you to understand this concept because it's a huge slap of reality for most people. Don't consider the amount of love you receive when reading this. Consider the amount of abuse you receive.

When I say, "*People meet you at the level that you have met yourself,*" I mean in all ways!

People also abuse you on the same level that you abuse yourself. When your partner refuses to "*listen to your needs*," you should consider where they learned that from.

YOU! You taught them that you were as unimportant as they are treating you. The truth is that we are always willing to put up with the same amount of abuse from someone else that we also give to ourselves. If someone is abusing you more than you abuse yourself, it feels "*wrong.*" If someone is abusing you less, it feels "*wrong.*"

Most relationships are predicated on two people acknowledging their fucked-up-ness together, and meeting each other at the same fucked up level, and remaining in this space for the duration of their relationship.

It's a "*I treat me like shit, you treat me like shit*" kind of arrangement that's never actually acknowledged, yet always adhered to.

I've been in relationships where people treated me like a queen, and it felt wildly uncomfortable. At the time, I didn't treat me as well as they did, and I bailed. It wasn't anything that reflected truth to me.

And on the other hand, I've had people who have tried to actually abuse me, and in those same situations, I've bailed. That's inconsistent with how I treat myself.

So here's ME...
I'm often insecure.
I have abandonment issues.
I question my self-worth.
I wonder if anyone truly loves me.
I don't think I'm good enough for someone to truly love.

So, if I'm in a relationship and someone is ignoring or dismissing me... CHECK – I ignore and constantly dismiss myself. It's fine. If I'm in a relationship and someone is refusing to be kind to me... CHECK – all good. I'm often unkind to myself.

See? All of these things feel "*familiar*" to me, so I accept them.

In my previous marriage, my spouse and I were equally bad to each other and equally good to each other... up until the end, where her level of emotional abuse became greater than the abuse I was willing to give myself.... and so I left.

She started making fun of my weight. She ridiculed me in public. She said things to me that were not consistent with how I felt about myself.

She said to a group of our common girlfriends that "*she deserved to be with someone else with a 27-inch waist like hers,*" and then would ridicule me publicly for not being that person. She would stand in front of me and say things like "*What is there to be attracted to? Look at you.*"

Yes, I had gained weight; but I hadn't yet gotten to the ultimate point of feeling as bad internally as she was attempting to shame me into feeling. And therefore, it all started feeling "*wrong*" to me. So I left.

As long as people are abusing us on a "*familiar*" level, we will tolerate it. However, the minute that abuse becomes more or less than ours, we feel uncomfortable and out of place.

And the abuse doesn't have to be an equal play for play. Perhaps he physically hits you, but you emotionally beat yourself up every day; so ultimately it leaves you with the same scars, same feelings, same issues.

Perhaps she takes you for granted and refuses to acknowledge what you do... but you allow it because you've spent a life time refusing to acknowledge your own greatness.

THE PROBLEM WITH RELATIONSHPS is that what we are externally searching for is someone to fulfill the things we haven't learned to give ourselves.

And the problem with this is.... it's not possible. It's not possible for someone to love you more than you've learned to love yourself. Do you know why? Because you don't recognize it anyway. It's pointless. You only recognize what you know, what you've learned to give yourself. What you've seen and experienced internally.

If you feel truly ugly... like truly unattractive, no amount of people complimenting you will matter. If you feel unworthy, there is no amount of someone telling you how happy they feel to be with you that will mean anything.

But these realities are all a part of the responsibility you're going to learn to take with this book.

You must stop being a victim, and you must take responsibility for the reality that YOU manifested all of the relationships in your life, all of the good and all of the bad, simply by the energy and truth within you.

You no longer get to say, *"He never treated me like I deserved."* YOU **NEVER TREATED YOU LIKE YOU DESERVED.**

All of the relationships in our life are learned behaviors. We **TEACH EVERYONE HOW TO TREAT US**. There is no exception to this rule. So if someone is treating you badly... it's because you've taught them that they can. And more likely than not, you didn't teach them with your words; you taught them with your actions.

You taught them that they can ignore your needs and feelings when you told them you needed something from them; and they ignored you, and you chose to stay with them.

In that moment, the abuse wasn't coming from them, it was coming from you. **YOU ARE ABUSING YOURSELF** and they are only mirroring that behavior.

You are your abuser.
You are your lover.
You are your counselor.
You are your very best friend.
You are your mom.
You are your dad.
You are the person who abandoned you.

And you are the person who is supposed to love you, forgive you, and be the most kind to you, always!

Make a promise to yourself from this point forward... that you will **NEVER** again say that you are a victim of someone else's actions towards you.

Responsibility will lead you to freedom.

Take responsibility for the fact that you showed them how to be despondent with you. You showed them how to ignore your needs. You showed them how to treat you as if you were less important than them. Again, they are only mirroring your actions. But fear not, there is hope here. I can help you fix all of these behaviors and relationships. But first...you MUST be willing to take responsibility.

Say it. Out loud.

"I am to blame, and I am to praise. I did this. I manifested this. I called this forth. I created this. But I also acknowledge that I have the power to change it all, instantly."

RULE #2

What we put up with, we end up with.

Anything you're willing to put up with from another person, any kind of behavior, anything at all, trust me when I say, you'll also end up with it.

There is no one who does something only twice. Once, totally possible. Twice? It's calculated and understood. No one will do something only twice. If they'll do it twice, they'll do it over and over and over.

So if you're putting up with repeated behavior, don't expect it to end. Plan for the reality that you'll be dealing with this shit for the duration of your relationship.

And if you're okay with it, be okay with it. But don't stay and bitch and hope that it changes. Nothing will change that you allow. That's just freaking crazy.

For the love of God, do not complain about something you've accepted more than once. It is your fault. You have created a space for this behavior to continue, and you alone have the power to change it simply by not accepting it.

RULE #3

You teach people how to treat you.

There is no exception to this rule. How your kids treat you. How your husband treats you. How your friends treat you. How your boss treats you. How your coworkers treat you. How your mom and dad treat you.... ALL OF IT is a learned behavior TAUGHT BY YOU.

Therefore if someone is treating you badly, it is your responsibility to re-teach them. And if they refuse to learn, then you must decide if you still want this person in your life. If you feel like it's mandatory that they're in your life no matter what, then my advice to you is that you make it mandatory that they re-learn how to treat you, period.

HOW TO RE-TRAIN SOMEONE TO TREAT YOU BETTER

Someone once wrote to me and said that her daughter was wildly disrespectful to her, and I was like, "*Why did you teach her that this was acceptable behavior?*"

Her response was that it was because she was going through a divorce and was feeling guilty. However, that was years ago, and now she's still treating her badly and she's not sure what to do.

Well, this is a perfect example of how you can re-train someone with truth and honesty.

My advice to her was to sit down with her daughter and explain **WHY** she accepted this unacceptable behavior to begin with. **THIS IS A VERY IMPORTANT PART.** You can't just suddenly "*change*" and then demand "*change*" around you. Nor should you demand change without explanation.

You must explain to the other human beings, who also have emotions (and memories), your processing and thinking.

This is the message I sent to her that I felt she should convey to her daughter:

"Honey, I need to talk to you. Cell phone off. I'd like for us to give one another some much-needed, undivided attention. I'm going to be very honest with you about a few things, and then I'd like to hear your honest feelings or opinion, no matter what that may be.

When your father and I separated I felt insanely guilty. I felt guilty because I came from a broken home and had promised myself that I'd never do that to my kids. I wanted nothing more than to raise you with two parents in your home and to make sure that you always felt loved, and secure. And when I realized that it wasn't an option for us to be together any longer, I felt so guilty.

And unfortunately, I allowed that guilt to dictate a large part of our relationship. I have allowed you to treat me disrespectfully out of guilt. But I love you too much, and I love me too much, to allow this to continue. It is imperative that you and I start respecting one another more; because it's imperative to me that we always know we have each other, no matter what. And the foundation for any sustainable relationship is respect.

So, first I need to apologize to you. I did this. I allowed it, and I'm sorry. Second, I need to create a new rule between us. You're no longer allowed to raise your voice at me, nor will I at you. You're no longer allowed to dismiss me when I'm speaking to you, nor will I you. Whenever we speak, let's make sure we "hear" each other and not just assume any longer.

I love you so much, and my relationship with you is so important to me that it's imperative that we change a few things. Now it's your turn to talk."

I wrote this out for this woman, who told me she basically did and said this verbatim. The response from her 14 year-old daughter was an apology, tears, hugs, and an hour of laughter and joy.

Kids are people too, with their own set of emotions and needs for all of the same things you do in life. Don't dismiss that.

I love the author Shari Storm, who wrote the book, "Motherhood Is The New MBA." In this book she explains how substantially imperative it is that you allow people the time and space to process **YOUR** changes, your feelings, your "*new rules,*" and your thoughts, etc. Don't just speak and expect an immediate understanding, resolution, or conclusion. She reminds us that it took us time to process this ourselves, and it's wildly unfair to expect someone to create understanding and resolution without the proper time to process on their own. And by the way, if you don't own this book, go buy it. It's great read!

She's right on the money. Yes, it's imperative that we understand that we teach people how to treat us; but it's also equally imperative that we allow them the time to process this change. "*Process*" as in a day or so, not months or years.

So, from this point forward, you're not allowed to complain.

RESPONSIBILITY IS KEY IN ALL RELATIONSHIPS

YOU ARE NOT A VICTIM OF ANYTHING OTHER THAN YOUR OWN CHOICES.

DOMESTIC VIOLENCE IS YOUR FAULT

How many of you just read that one line and you got super pissed? I would challenge you to stop being so emotionally reactionary, and keep reading.

You know by now that I'm not a sugar-coating writer. I know if you're getting physically abused that you're going to truly disdain these words. But if you'll be willing to look past the emotional response, and truly consider the truth that I'm bringing to your awareness, this may actually **SAVE YOUR LIFE.**

Domestic abuse counselors often get this one wrong too. They create too much of a *"victim"* mentality for women who are in abusive relationships. They continue to cultivate this idea that they're helpless by using language like *"you're not in control, he is,"* or *"none of this is your fault,"* as if to insinuate that they are 100% helpless.

I'm going to give you another, much less popular perspective, and tell you that it is **NOT** your fault he hit you once, but there is a level of personal responsibility you must take for staying in a relationship after that moment.

He hit you and he apologized; and you wanted so badly to maintain the other elements of your relationship that you chose to stay. And then the cycle began...

This scenario places you in a position of needing to take some responsibility, and from that responsibility I believe you can actually empower yourself to get out.

The constant barrage of "*victimhood*" is actually disempowering to you; and anyone who allows you to stay in that space is doing you a huge disservice.

ABUSED KIDS HAVE A HIGH TOLERANCE FOR ABUSE AS ADULTS.

This is just a fact of life. We end up becoming conditioned by the abuse and used to it.

It's why when I was 16 years old, my boss convinced me that it was okay to take naked pictures of me – because I had, at this point, already suffered so much abuse that it didn't seem that bad to stand in front of a camera and let a 40-year old man violate me. At least he wasn't assaulting me physically.

My tolerance level for abuse was at an all-time high by the time I had reached my late teenage years; and I continued to attract abusers throughout my 20's. And they were all as drawn to me, as I was to them.

IT IS NOT OKAY FOR SOMEONE TO HIT YOU

In my 20's, I got into a relationship where someone hit me and I didn't leave them. Hitting me didn't really feel like that big of a deal... I just spent my childhood learning that this is just how some people express themselves when they're angry.

But hitting you is 100% unacceptable. **IT IS A BIG DEAL.** It is not something that you should ever overlook, or chalk up to a bad day, or a crappy moment, and then continue to stay in a relationship with.

The entire point to this section is to highlight your own responsibility in this situation if you choose to do that. If you are getting abused and choosing to ignore it, you must take responsibility for where you are!

If he beats you, but he's otherwise a great provider for you and your children, you are actively choosing to stay in an abusive situation so that you can enjoy the other elements of this relationship. **YOU ARE NOT A VICTIM.** You are a perpetrator in your own life. You are abusing yourself by allowing yourself to get abused.

I have a friend whose husband, every once in a blue moon, will go out with his friends and drink. Several times he has come home and hit her. And then she parades her black eyes around town as proof of the fact that she's a victim. Every. Single. Time. But she's not a victim of anything but her own decision to stay.

Sadly, she will say really stupid shit like, "*If he's not drinking though he's great, and we are great. I just need him to stop drinking.*" But she's never demanded that he does. She's never even given him an ultimatum. She just complains when it happens, and then eventually it's chalked up to "*a bad moment*" – until the next one...

I would strongly encourage you to honestly reflect on why you choose to stay, and begin the healing process there. Perhaps you don't feel good enough at the core of you, and you're afraid that "*this is all there is for you.*" You can fix this abusive relationship simply by healing yourself. Because the truth is that **IF** you would take the time to self-reflect and truly heal and grow through this, the next time he hit you, you'd be out the door before he ever had the chance to apologize.

At the core of an abused woman is usually a very frightened, insecure little girl who lacks some serious self-esteem. Heal that little girl and watch the woman grow out of this relationship!

THE TRUTH ABOUT RELATIONSHIPS

People will only meet you in life at the same level in which you've been willing to meet yourself. You know what happened when I finally started growing inwardly and realizing the implicit truth within me that I was a spiritual giant and a badass human being?

Suddenly all of the relationships around me started reflecting this level of depth. I fell in love with someone who met me at this epic level of self-awareness. I started suddenly attracting deeper, far more meaningful friendships.

If you're being really honest with yourself you can see right now that all of the relationships around you reflect the relationship you have within you.

If you're only "*kind of*" honest with yourself, you'll find that others will be "kind of" honest with you back. If you're wildly self-forgiving, you'll find that others will be as equally forgiving. If you're constantly berating yourself, putting yourself down, and dismissing your own feelings, then you will discover that those closest to you will also mirror these destructive behaviors.

EVERYONE WILL TAKE YOUR LEAD

If you're being abused, or used, or mistreated, or discarded in any way, consider how you're doing this to yourself first, instead of taking the normal path of finger-pointing and deflection.

I once sent someone a heartfelt email, which took me hours to author, only to have them call me and say, "I'm not going to bother reading your email. I don't care."

The email was about how I felt like they had been dismissing my feelings, and how I had felt this way for a long time, and that I would appreciate it if they would consider where I was coming from.

I actually laughed out loud at the reality of this truth in front of me. The Universe had just sat up a huge mirror in front of me that said "WHY SHOULD SHE CARE ABOUT YOUR FEELINGS WHEN YOU DON'T?"

The truth is that I was expecting someone to give me something I wasn't even willing to give myself. And that's just a nutty freaking concept altogether.

I walked away from this experience calling them selfish, telling them (and others) how horrible they were to me... constantly berating them for treating me badly. How dare you not respect me?

Yet, I never left the relationship. I never demanded anything more. I only bitched.

The truth is that this person simply met me where I was meeting myself. They didn't do anything to me that I wasn't already doing. They were simply mirroring my own actions towards myself.

Everyone will meet you right where you are.
They'll abuse you like you abuse you.
They'll love you like you love you.
They'll respect you like you respect you.
And yes, they'll dismiss you, as you dismiss you.

The irony in this story is now hilarious to me. I mean, I sent someone a freaking email asking them not to dismiss me, and they called to tell me they received it but didn't care enough to read it.

Hilarious! Hilarious actually ONLY because I was able to see the truth for what it was eventually.

This wasn't their fault. They aren't to blame.

I mean, for one, YES, this person no longer deserves to be in my life; but more importantly I have discovered the truth within myself.

They poked an open wound that already existed within me and mirrored my own self-abuse, and I blamed them all the way to the bank. I blamed them until I learned the lesson above. Everyone treats us the same way we treat ourselves.

In order for me to create relationships where people don't automatically dismiss me, I must first learn to stop dismissing myself.

Same with you.

It is literally an act of total insanity to expect someone to treat you better than you're treating yourself. It's a ludicrous thought to assume that someone will respect you in ways that you don't already respect yourself.

I would strongly encourage you to consider the relationships in your life that feel like they hurt the most, and honestly reflect on how those people are simply holding up a mirror of yourself in some capacity. They are only reflecting what you're already doing to yourself.

"WHEN YOU CRIED IT ACTUALLY TURNED ME ON MORE"

I met with a woman once who told me that her husband had approached her about having a threesome. Yes, a threesome – as in bringing someone else into their marriage and having sex.

She was disappointed at first. She had no desire to do it, but she didn't want to seem like a prude to her husband. She's also thinking that if she does this for him, he will respect, love, and want her more. She was also assuming that the threesome is with another woman.

When she finally responded to him and said that she would agree to the threesome, he conveys that his fantasy is not with another woman but with another man. His biggest fantasy was to see another man having sex with his wife.

She was completely caught off guard, and this hurt her heart to hear this. She was shocked.

She continued to tell me that she had always given in to him. Anything he ever wanted, she gave. Anything he needed, she did. All things outside of all of her comfort zones, all to please him.

She continued explaining that she believed he was a "*better catch*" than she was. He was handsome. He was charming. She was neither. She had always approached their relationship as if she was the "*lucky one*." And he had always known this, and he had always treated her as such.

After years of dismissing and disrespecting her (and her allowing it), it eventually became a fantasy of his to watch someone else actually disrespect her.

Her deep-seeded level of insecurity, lack of self-worth, and blatant disregard for her own feelings had gotten so out of hand within her that the mirrored seeds of destruction started presenting themselves all around her.

The deliberate indifference she had for herself was being mirrored on such a tantamount level by her husband that he actually started getting creative in order to meet her at this level of disrespect and self-hatred.

That's seriously nuts. I mean...that's insanely, seriously NUTS! And... as you can imagine, she let him have his fantasy.

He found another man who met her at a bar at a local hotel. He watched as they flirted, and then he snuck up into the hotel room and he sat in the corner as they walked in and he undressed her. With tears streaming down her face, she allowed this man to pound her with one single fucking thrust of self-hatred after the next. And she cried tears of pain as her husband watched, masturbating the entire time.

And you know what he said afterwards? The "*crying part*" actually made it a bigger turn-on for him.

WHEN SHE CRIED, IT TURNED HIM ON MORE...

So let's break this down... Why did she do this? Because she wanted to please him, as she says? No chance.

She did it because her level of self-worth was at an all-time low, below zero, as was her insecurity. And she didn't believe that she deserved better.

Bad, awful, abusive, horrible love sometimes feels better than no love. Because NO LOVE means we are left alone to discover the truths within ourselves; and more often than not, THOSE TRUTHS hurt worse than the abuse we have become accustomed to endure.

She had gotten to a point of self-abusing so deeply that she was allowing a consensual rape to take place. And yes, this act is exactly what I would call "consensual rape."

WHAT IS CONSENUAL RAPE?

CONSENSUAL RAPE happens when someone isn't strong enough to say no, but they have no desire to have sex; and the person who is having sex with them is all too aware of this reality, yet does it anyway.

THIS IS CONSENSUAL RAPE. It happens all the time.

Women with daddy issues who are afraid to disappoint the men in their lives often find themselves in this situation. They have no desire to have sex, yet he's pressuring her. And he knows she will not deny him, because at the core of her is a deep-seeded lack of self-love and worth.

"DADDY ISSUES" LEAD TO *"HUSBAND ISSUES"*

I actually had a male friend of mine tell me, after his recent divorce, that he's not looking for commitment. He's actually just looking for some girls with some deep-seeded daddy issues who can't say *"no"* to him.

My natural inclination was to yell at him and berate him for this wildly fucked-up comment. Instead, however, in a quick moment of clarity, I said, "Exactly how insecure are you, my friend?"

And you know what came out of the wildly-enlightening conversation that then took place? He explained that he seeks women with daddy issues, because deep down inside he's got some serious freaking mommy issues.

He doesn't feel "*good enough*" to be with a woman who has her shit together, so (call it what you want) he's really just looking for someone as fucked up as he is, as lost as he is, and as in need of someone filling the voids in his life that he can't seem to figure out how to fill.

He continues to state that it feels good to be with someone who fills the voids within him every now and then, and makes him feel worthy.

But herein lies the biggest problem of all. If it feel like someone is actually "*filling a void*" within you, the truth is that they're only masking it. And the problem with masking it is that when it's not addressed it becomes bigger and more painful. And once that Band-Aid is ripped off, it will feel more overwhelming and emotionally agonizing than ever before.

This is how people get "*lost*" in relationships. They don't lose themselves as much as they actually lose perspective. They have forgotten that the point of being in a relationship isn't to have someone fix what's wrong with you or to put Band-Aids over all of the broken pieces, it's to add to the greatness of what you're already feeling.

They're the icing, not the cake. Too many people make their relationships the cake, and when the cake walks out the door, they drop to their knees as if they're going to starve for the rest of their lives, feeling more lost than before.

TRUST ME WHEN I SAY THIS:

If you are relying on anyone to make you feel something you're not able to make yourself feel, there will be a reckoning one day. You will be forced to see the truth for what it is.

You'll discover that they weren't actually making you feel anything at all; they were simply masking the void within you and allowing you to evade the truth that exists there.

DEAR MEN WHO SEEK "WEAKER" WOMEN:

I know that deep down inside this isn't actually the relationship you want to be in. I know that you are acting out of insecurity and feeling powerless over yourself and your own life. I know that it temporarily makes you feel better to be able to be with someone who ignores all that you feel is wrong with you, as you do. And that to be able to possess power over someone else is an incredible way to mask the reality that you feel as though you don't have power over yourself.

However, this cycle of using others and abusing yourself will only continue to grow stronger until it one day feels overwhelmingly too powerful to end.

It could also potentially cause you to become abusive in your relationships, as the need to abuse also derives the same foundation of not feeling worthy.

Please do yourself a favor and begin to reflect on the things that have brought you to this awareness. There is a greater man within you, waiting for you to acknowledge him. And this man isn't attracted to women who reflect his weakness, but more so attracted to a woman who reflects his strength and individuality. Find that man.

YOU ALONE HOLD THE POWER
No one can make you feel *"good enough."* They can sometimes temporarily make you forget that you don't feel worthy, but they're not actually making you feel *"good enough."*

No one can make you feel attractive, actually. They can sometimes temporarily mask the reality that you feel ugly, but in the end, it's not them who can change how you feel about yourself.

And if someone says something that resonates with you, good or bad, you will take it to heart. And you will praise them or you will blame them, but the truth is that NONE OF it is real.

However, the truth lies within you. How you feel is how you feel. People come and go, and they are reminders of this; and sometimes those reminders feel good and sometimes they feel awful. But it is never about them.

Make a promise to yourself right now that you will change the line *"You made me feel..."* to *"you just reminded me that I feel..."* It will empower you and start the process of removing blame outside of yourself, which in return can begin the healing process much faster.

HE CHEATED. AND NOW HE'S DEFEATED...
I recently spoke to a couple who just went through an *"infidelity"* issue. He cheated on her, but apologized profusely, stating that it was a situational thing, and asked for forgiveness. After months of therapy she decided to take him back.

However, after she took him back, the relationship didn't start over from a new perspective as he had hoped for. She only took him back, as he later discovered, so that she could punish him.

She started berating him, not just privately but also in front of their friends. She would demand access to all of his private things: emails, cell phone, etc. She told him he was no longer allowed to go out with his buddies until she felt comfortable enough to allow it to happen. And she basically "*grounded him*," as you would a child in their own home.

He accepted this behavior, however, because (obviously) he felt guilty, and allowing this abuse was his penance.

However, years went by and this abuse is still happening. She's still treating him badly in public and speaking to him like he's a two-year old out of control. She's still demanding that he has no privacy from her and rarely lets him go out. If he does go out, she contacts him every 30 minutes in an effort to maintain control over him. And he's now at a point where he no longer wants to be in this relationship.

Much like how I became someone who was distant with the world around me because I had been raised in a home with distance.... this woman did the exact same thing. **She became the thing that hurt her. She mirrored the pain by being the pain instead of dealing with the pain.**

If you refuse to deal with the core issue at hand, and instead flippantly dismiss the deeper truths within you, you will find yourself doing the same thing. You will become the pain, and therefore become the abuser, the cheater, the one who hurts others with your dissidence and selfishness. And in the end you will realize you are no different than those who have caused you the most pain in life.

She took advantage of her husband's sorrow, sadness, and regret and used it as an opportunity to abuse him with it.

He contacted me and told me this story and said, "*I no longer want to be with her. She has broken me down to a point that I no longer respect her or even care about her need to resent me.*"

Here was my advice to him. I encouraged him to write his wife this letter: "*I love you, but I am really having some issues with how I am being treated in our marriage. The truth is that I felt so disgusted with myself after I cheated on you, and so hurt FOR YOU by what I had done, and so full of guilt, that I allowed you to punish me by treating me badly.*

However, a great deal of time has passed, and I have given you ample time to choose forgiveness and moving forward. But you continue to keep us in that moment that broke us down. I feel like you're refusing to allow us to move past this because of your need to continue to punish me. And I can't keep living a life where someone is berating me and punishing me for something I did a long time ago.

If you want to be with me, you have to either move past this moment or you need to be very honest with me and admit that you're not ready to. I love you. And I will never do what I did again. And when you chose to stay with me, you chose to believe this. So now I need your actions to reflect this. Trust is imperative between us; and yes, I know I broke that bond, but I must be forgiven and we must move forward.

I want you to spend some time thinking about how you feel about all of this and truthfully determining whether or not you're ready to truly forgive and trust me again."

The conversation ended with her admitting that she would never trust him again; and as long as they were together, she would need to "*control*" him because she doesn't believe him. And he chose to walk away... rightfully so.

If someone isn't willing to meet you where you deserve to be met, you must be willing to walk away. I suspect I don't need to remind you of what happens when you draw lines in the sand and allow people to cross them.

When love is no longer being served at the table, it is no longer your table!

DISRESPECT TURNS INTO ABUSE WHEN THERE ARE NO BOUNDARIES.

It's like my favorite cartoon growing up, where Bugs Bunny continues to draw so many lines in the ground that Elmer exclaims over and over he will not cross... yet continues to cross... and eventually he ends up falling off the side of the cliff and dying. Why? Because he was allowing someone to disrespect him and blatantly erase boundaries that he needed for the relationship.

It's a cartoon – that is a strange reality of life. How many times have you asked someone to not do something, or "*to*" do something, that they blatantly refused to act on? If you're being honest with this, you'll also notice that they're behavior towards you had grown increasingly more and more disrespectful. This is the result of you not respecting your own boundaries and needs. It shows up in front of you.

The world around you is a mirror image of all that is within you.

WHO IS MAKING THE DECISIONS HERE?

Behind every single decision your make is an underling agenda and emotion. Making your kids dinner every night, ironing your husband's shirts before work, refusing to give the new guy at work a chance to really get to know him, going on a diet, going on vacation... every single decision you make in life comes with a purposeful hidden agenda behind it.

So, looking back on many of our crazy life choices, we can follow the line all the way back to the core issue.

I discovered something very enlightening about myself recently. And that it is that I personally rarely ever make a decision in my life from a feeling of wholeness, thoughtfulness, or true understanding of what it means.

Just hear me out here... What I discovered is that when we make decisions about something, anything actually, there's usually an underlying feeling involved making the decision for us. And there's not only an underlying emotion, there's an overall agenda that is attached to that emotion.

For instance, when some man is treating you badly, and you know you deserve so much better than the fresh horse shit he's feeding you, yet you still continue to put up with him, there's an underlying agenda within you to not feel lonely in the moment, and the feeling making the decision is "*fear.*"

Imagine a better, stronger, more put together, greater version of the human being you are today... you know better, you've seen better, you're absolutely certain that you are deserving of great things... and in that light, the next time someone comes by to treat you badly, you walk off, you dismiss them as crazy.

I think one of the most interesting things to consider in life is **WHICH** one of your emotions made each of the decisions that led you down each path in life. Call your emotions out by each of their names.

There's fear. There's insecurity. There's doubt. There's worry. There's love. There's hope. There's faith. The list is endless... And all of these emotions within you are separate entities inside of you, motivating you to move in one direction or another.

I often talk to my emotions, as if they're people living inside of me. Whenever I'm feeling forced to make a certain decision, I always take a step back, reflect within, and ask, *"Which one of you is trying to make this decision?"*

Was it hope and love that got me into my first marriage? Or was it doubt and fear? Was it the idea that I had fallen in love and believed wholly that I had finally found my counterpart in life? Or was it the fear that I was getting older? Was it loneliness? Was it hopelessness making the decision after facing many pointless dates and uneventful nights with others along the way?

Who makes most of your decisions? Who is making the decision to stay at your job that makes you feel unfulfilled? Who is making the decision to keep you in that marriage? Who is making the decision to go to marriage counseling? Who does most of the decision making within you?

It's a question you should ask yourself and truly consider, daily, as you go through each of your actions. **WHO** is making this decision?

Through most of my 20's, doubt, fear, and insecurity made most of the decisions. I can look back now and see that it was very infrequent that a decision was made out of truly feeling *"whole"* and *"healthy"* about it. It was always, *"I'll stay in this shit-hole relationship because bad love feels better than no love."* It was fear that kept me lying to people about who I was as a human being, because *"No one would ever really love me if they truly knew me."* It was insecurity that had sex, because I was convinced that sex meant I was attractive. And at least for a moment I wasn't ugly anymore. It was loneliness that continued to allow people to abuse me and treat me badly, and I kept coming back for more and more and more.

I have worn my heart on my sleeve my entire life, thinking that if people can see the vulnerable side of me, they'll be less likely to hurt me. But it doesn't matter if you wear your heart out or not. People are who they are, regardless of what you do.

PART 7.

THE CALMING TRUTH

WAS THAT REALLY A MISTAKE?

If you ask most people what their most epic mistake in life was, they'll more likely tell you it was *"marrying that person that ended in disaster,"* or *"dating that dude who turned out to be the world's biggest douche canoe,"* or *"starting that business that failed"* or *"buying that thing that ended up feeling more like a noose around my neck than it did a blessing."*

If you were to look back on your life, what would you say was the single worst decision you've ever made? Really think about it.

STOP RIGHT HERE and THINK.

Now I want you to erase everything that happened in your life **AFTER** that decision, and tell me if you feel like it was still a *"mistake."* You married a douche canoe – but you had amazing kids. If you're going to take away the mistake, you have to take away the kids too.

You put all of your money into a new business and had to file for bankruptcy. But that's where you met that new business contact who gave you another great opportunity that led you down a cooler path. Or perhaps it's just where you learned a shit ton of business lessons that have made you a wildly powerful and invaluable employee/employer elsewhere.

Maybe you bought a house and lost it all to the recession. But going through that experience brought you to a new awareness about yourself and your inner strength, resolve, and resilience.

If you want to call it a mistake, you have to erase what happened after. So maybe you didn't lose your home to foreclosure, but you also aren't as strong as you are today.

I only say all of this because I know a lot of people spend their lives beating the fuck out of themselves over what they perceive to be mistakes in life.

"*IF ONLY*" are two simple words that will kill you, your spirit, and your will to live (and grow and thrive).

As many "*mistakes*" as I feel like I've made, I also realize that it was **ALL** just a bunch of experiences I need to personally have to create this woman I am today. If not for all of the above, I would be nothing like I am today. So... as with all good communication that needs to take place in the beginning of all significant relationships, let's begin by defining our collective language together.

There are no mistakes in this world. There are no accidents in the Universe. There isn't anything you weren't supposed to experience that you ended up experiencing.

So when I say "*mistake*" I only mean it in the "*that's what you keep calling that decision*" kind of way... but I'm about to show you otherwise. ;)

What takes most people down in life is NOT what actually happens, but their perception of what happened.

Perspective is everything.
And besides all of this, let's be really honest here: the only reason you've hung this noose around your neck filled with the "*woulda, shoulda, and coulda's*" is because of the expectations you had going into the situation.

You assumed that the relationship would last a lifetime. So when it didn't you flipped the hell out. You assumed that your business wasn't just a '*stepping stone*' but treated it more like some kind of an arrival platform, so when you had to close shop you flipped the hell out.

ASSUMPTIONS & EXPECTATIONS ARE THE ROOT OF ALL OF OUR SUFFERING.

- Both of these things have ruined my life.
- They have killed great relationships.
- They have ruined what could have been great experiences.
- They have led me into murky, shark-infested waters where I was barely able to escape alive (I mean this quite literally).
- They have precluded me from being able to enjoy so much that could have otherwise just been an amazing love or experience.

And it is these two evil words that are at the root of the word "*mistake.*" It only seemed like a mistake because of your expectations and assumptions. Had you gone into that situation without any perceived outcome, you would have just gone with the flow of how it all played out for you.

So this is what I learned from my beautiful, healing, amazing, soulful, great friend, artist, life coach, Sufi, hell-of-a-human-being, Julia Junkin....

"... THAT WHICH HITS YOU COULD NEVER HAVE MISSED YOU."

Write that down on your bathroom mirror, and **stop acting like you could have re-routed yourself around that life lesson.** You couldn't have anyway. No matter how it played out, it would have played out with that "*mistake*" in it.

Have you ever read the book, "*The Afterlife of Billy Fingers?*" It's a great book to read for those of you who have lost loved ones close to you.

The gist of the book is that this dude who was a drug addict dies. After he dies, he comes back and visits his sister and tells her all about the afterlife he's experiencing.

It sounds crazy, as I'm trying to relegate this epic book's greatness into this simple explanation; but trust me, it's worth the read.

In the book, Billy states that there is a moment after you die where you can go back and see your whole life – not on display for everyone to judge, but alone. You can see all of the decisions you made, and you can see why, from a clearer and deeper perspective, you chose certain paths.

But one of the biggest *"take aways"* for me in the book was Billy stating that he realized that **ALL roads he could have taken STILL LED HIM TO ALL OF THE SAME PLACES. Every single possible option led him to each pivotal moment he experienced.**

As he flirted with the idea of *"What would have happened had I married her instead?"* He still became a drug addict. He still wrecked his car. He still lost that job. He still fucked up in all of the same ways. No matter what different roads he entertained, or how many decisions he made different, in the end he still ended up in every pivotal moment in the same way.

I found that reality to be so empowering.

Why? Because we are here to learn our personal life lessons that we were sent here to learn. Because (as the Sufi's say) **THAT WHICH HIT YOU COULD NEVER HAVE MISSED YOU.**

WE ARE SPIRITUAL BEINGS HAVING A HUMAN EXPERIENCE!

Our spirits are here having this "*human*" experience. Every single religion in the world agrees that we are spiritual beings. I mean, the only way you can argue that reality (no matter what religion you follow) is if you're an atheist. However, I suspect that if you are, you're probably not very drawn to my writing... so essentially **EVERYONE** reading this has to agree with the fact that we are spiritual beings having a human experience. Don't mix that up. Don't turn that around. Don't act like the reason you're here is some surface, human, shallow need to look good and get laid and do blow off some hooker's ass or make lots of money, or whatever...

So, let's start the evaluation of our lives by realizing how much our thinking, and defining, and expecting, and assuming, has gotten us into this trouble... not in life, but in our minds.

IT DOESN'T LOOK LIKE THAT FROM THIS PERSPECTIVE

That's what God is thinking (or the spirits are thinking) as they're all looking down, and all around you. They can see behind you and ahead of you. **And as you're thinking everything is falling apart, what you don't realize is that it's all actually falling perfectly into place for you.**

The whole Universe is conspiring FOR YOU. Seriously.

It's never falling apart. It's always falling perfectly into place for you. It's just that you've got a sick case of tunnel vision and can't see beyond your own assumptions and expectations.

So never ever again are you allowed to call something a mistake. The only mistake is you calling it a mistake. And never again are you allowed to ever think, "*It wasn't supposed to be like this, or go like this, or end up like this.*"

It was supposed to go as it went.

He was supposed to leave.
She was supposed to die.
They were supposed to move away.
You were supposed to be let go so you could move on.
You were supposed to be alone in that moment.
In this moment.

IN any moment that is happening, it's **ALL** conspiring for you!

Write that down on your bathroom mirror.

LOS ANGELES TO NEW YORK CITY

Did you know you can drive from Los Angeles, California, all the way to New York City without seeing more than just a few feet in front of you at a time? You don't see New York City while you're driving, as motivation to keep driving. Irrespective of the fact that you can only see what's directly in front of you, **YOU KEEP DRIVING.**

In fact, when driving, we rarely see our final destination in sight. We drive out of faith. We know that no matter how many potholes we may hit along the way, how many detours may change our route, no matter how many breakdowns or unexpected stops along the way, we still keep driving because we are absolutely, undeniably certain that **WHERE** we are **GOING** exists. And nothing can stop us from getting there. We may change courses. We may end up switching cars, and flying half the way. But one way or another, we are going to get there.

When was the last time you went somewhere in life with THAT kind of faith and tenacity?

This is the reality that got me to drive up to that college and ask for an interview. That job was my New York City, and I couldn't see more than 2 feet in front of me at that time, but I knew it existed, and I wasn't about to stop driving there just because some lady on the other end of a cell phone told me no.

So, tell me. Are you more likely to be the person who listens to the "*no's*" and walks away? Or are you the person who creates your own reality all around you and stops at nothing to see your dreams come true?

Most of our greatest opportunities in life are brilliantly disguised as challenges and problems.

YOU ARE LITERALLY BEING EATEN ALIVE

Do you know the actual details of what has to happen inside the internal organs of a caterpillar in order for it to transform into a butterfly? The story is unbelievably empowering.

At the very beginning of the transformation stage, the internal cells inside a caterpillar begin to battle. They literally battle cells known as "*imaginal cells*" and are actually fighting to stay while the new cells are fighting to take over.

In this epic battle, as the new imaginal cells begin to win, they begin to break down the actual internal structure of this creature, literally turning it into an unrecognizable goo-like structure, totally broken down. And then eventually, when the imaginal cells completely win this epic battle, the butterfly begins to emerge.

There is literally no difference at all between you and a caterpillar fighting to turn into a butterfly.

I think one of the most prolific life lessons in this is the one that's always overlooked: It is not the caterpillar who wants to transform, but rather the butterfly that wants to take over.

Why is this important? Because the "*you*" as you are today does not hold the power to do anything. You must completely surrender to this new being. It is not you who will win this battle, but a whole new version of yourself in the end that will emerge from the ashes.

THE WHOLE UNIVERSE IS CONSPIRING FOR YOU.

PART 8.

TOOLS AND TRUTHS FOR MOVING FORWARD

WOULD YOU STILL BE POOR?

I heard someone say once that if all of the wealth in the world were evenly distributed among everyone in the United States, that within 10 to 20 years all of the same rich people would be rich and all of the same poor people would be poor. I'm not sure who told me this, but I can't stop contemplating the concept and wonder if there is some truth to this.

The reality is that this financial hypothesis of wealth distribution coincides with everything I believe about **life and have always said... that life is about conditioning, and all that we have** *"put up with"* **we will end up with – NOT out of a series of cognitive daily choices, but rather a life-long belief system that lives within us.**

WHY ARE YOU HERE?

There is only one you on this planet... and there's a reason why you are here. And that reason is not to live some mediocre life and barely get by. Your reason for being alive isn't to pay bills and live in depression, or fear, or sadness, or regret.

RISE. AND RISE AGAIN. For you are powerful beyond your own understanding. And you are standing on this earth because you have something to bring to this world in a way that no one else can.

SING IT. SAY IT. PLAY IT. WRITE IT. DO IT. RAISE IT. LOVE IT. KEEP IT. MAKE IT. DANCE IT. HOLD IT. CREATE IT.

SELF WORTH IS KEY

You have been conditioned to believe that you aren't good enough to make a million dollars. You dismiss it all together. As if...

In your mind, that kind of wealth only happens to the *"lucky"* ones, or those born with a silver spoon in their mouth, or those blessed with better looks or talent, or just anyone else in the world but you. You live by a belief system that you will never be *"them."* And therefore, like the elephant, you don't even entertain the idea anymore.

A good friend of mine, author and life-coach, Kris Prochaska, always reminds me that *"we are constantly looking for evidence in life to support our belief systems."* Everywhere we go, every conversation we have, every single one of our experiences only highlights that we are correct.

This is why many people who grow up in poverty end up staying in poverty. They have learned (through conditioning) that fortune and success isn't possible for them, so they don't even bother trying. And they spend the majority of their adult life proving to themselves that they're not good enough. Anything they can find to support the belief that they'll never have more feels comfortable, and accurate.

Les Brown says, *"It's not that most people aim high and miss, it's that they aim low and hit."* Then they get stuck. You never even tried to have more... because you have been conditioned to believe that THIS. IS. IT.

WHY NOT ME? WHY NOT YOU?

I live my life by 3 simple words, every single day: **WHY NOT ME?**

Did you know there are people right now who are making a weekly salary of what you're hoping to make yearly? Your annual dream is their weekly reality.

The truth is that there is abundance flowing all around you. There is more money in this world than this world needs. And there are people all over planet Earth overindulging in that abundance as we speak. They're living the dream... your dreams too actually, and theirs. They're traveling the world, and experiencing life, and seeing things you only see in a movie theater or read in books.

What makes them able to live like this while the rest of the world is living one paycheck away from total poverty (if not otherwise already there)?

ARE YOU BLOCKING YOURSELF FROM FINANCIAL FREEDOM?

Most people don't realize that **THEY** are blocking their own financial freedom. They are the problem. If you have spent a life with "*money problems,*" that you don't realize you've perpetuated them into your future. Just those two words in themselves create poverty. Money isn't a problem, YOU are. You've created the inability to attract abundance. You have blocked financial freedom. You are the one focusing on "*barely enough...*" so much so that you wouldn't even know what abundance looked like if it was staring you in the face. You've been conditioned to believe that you'll always struggle financially, and therefore every single thing you do only continues to perpetuate this reality for you.

Most people don't realize how much of their energy and attitude about money attracts a negative experience. If you're standing around thinking about all of the things that you're going to do with your entire paycheck before you even get it, you've attracted more financial poverty. If you're worrying about how the bills are going to get paid, you've only brought on more things to worry about. Trust me... more bills are on their way.

It's like the energy of abundance and financial wealth is floating above you, sees all of your negative shit and energy, and decides to just keep floating on by. It isn't attracted to you and all of your "*money problems.*"

Abundance isn't attracted to it's opposite. It actually can't even find you with your poverty mentality.

In the same way that "*like energy attracts itself,*" so does money. Abundance attracts abundance. This is why I always say, "*Those who say thank you will always have the most to say thank you for.*" Gratitude is a mentality that energetically attracts positive situations. When you're feeling stuck, you're exuding energy of frustration, anger, resentment, sadness, poverty, etc... and therefore only attracting more of all of the above to your front door in life.

When you're feeling an overwhelming sense of gratitude, hope, faith, love, kindness, giddiness, etc, you're attracting more of that too.

LIVING WITH PURPOSE

Nearly a century ago, journalist Napoleon Hill studied over 500 self-made millionaires. His interviews and research culminated in the 1937 bestseller, "*Think and Grow Rich*," one of my all time favorite books (which I highly recommend you read if you haven't yet).

In the book, Napoleon states that the starting point of all achievement is "*Definiteness of Purpose.*" According to Hill, it's the single most important principle he learned from all of his years of studying hundreds and hundreds of rags-to-riches stories of self-made millionaires all over the world.

He states that you absolutely must know what you want before you can get it. I find this to be fascinating, considering most people live their lives on autopilot, never really considering this question at all.

What's the end game here? What is it that you want to be, to build, to have, to see, to do? What does it look like exactly? Do you know? Or are you just living life on autopilot, being blown wherever the wind takes you in life, and using words like "*some day,*" and "*maybe,*" and "*if I'm lucky enough,*" or (yikes) "*If it's the Lord's will for me...*"

When was the last time you actually lived with intention?

Me? Hardly ever. This is why I found this book so fascinating. I mean, I wholeheartedly believe that I can create any reality I want for my own life. I believe that I have the power to manifest anything I desire... yet I rarely live intentionally. I have no clue what the end game is for me with most things, and I certainly don't know what I want to get out of life.

But this was one of the important common denominators Hill found existed in all of these **SELF-MADE** millionaires. Intentional living.

30-DAY "INTENTIONAL-LIVING" CHALLENGE

AT THIS POINT IN THE BOOK YOU SHOULD STOP READING AND ASK YOURSELF THESE QUESTIONS:

1. What do you want in life?
2. Who do you want to be?
3. How do you want to be remembered?
4. What mark do you want to leave on this planet?
5. What do you want your life to look like in one year, or five years, ten years?
6. What's the end game here for you?

Write it all down, and be specific. Don't use generic words and phrases like *"I just want to be happy,"* or *"I just want to be rich."* That's bullshit, and generic goals create generic results.

Be specific and as detailed as possible.

I want this book to become a best-seller. I want to be asked to speak at venues all over the world about its content. And I want to be known as someone who helped changed the world by helping to shape individual lives all over the planet. I want to bring awareness to people of how amazing they are and illuminate their epic potential in a way that they've never known before. I want people to sit down and read this book and let it be the catalyst that ultimately causes true growth and personal development.

Someone the other day told me that she describes me to her husband as *"the female Tony Robins."* I don't want to be known as that. I want to be known as a dynamic, engaging, inspiring, and motivating public speaker and author; one that's different than anything the world stage has ever seen before. I don't want to be Tonia Robbins. I want to be Kristy Sinsara.

I mean, don't get me wrong, Tony Robbins is a mega giant of a badass human being. **I LOVE HIM.** But I don't want to be him.

The end game for me looks like me standing on a stage with a few thousand people in front of me, and me being able to bring my own personal gifts to this table in life, and leave this life knowing I held nothing back. I left nothing behind me. I conquered all that I could conquer.

I want to walk off a stage and have a woman walk up to me and tell me that something I wrote, something I said, something I did, motivated her to change her entire life or inspired her to grow in ways she never knew possible. **THAT IS MY END GAME.**

I'm living it already. **THIS IS MY DREAM.**

What's yours?
Be crazy. Be honest. Be specific.
I want my book to become a best seller within 6 months of publishing it. I want to be on a worldwide book tour reading it out loud to people all over the planet.

I SAY GO FOR CRAZY GOALS and beat the odds. Do the things you're not supposed to be able to do and create new limitations for humanity.

FINDING EPIC GREATNESS

THE TRUTH ABOUT "THE SECRET"

I love the book, "*The Secret.*" It's one of the books that has helped shape and mold so much of the thought patterns and belief systems in my life. The overall concept of the book is simply explaining "*The Law of Attraction.*"

Basically the Law of Attraction says that you attract into your life all of the things, circumstances, and conditions that correspond with the nature of your dominant, habitual thoughts and beliefs, both conscious and subconscious. I like to say, "*Your life is a sum of all of your subconscious beliefs.*" The basic premise of the Law of Attraction is that "*like energy attracts like energy.*" And, according to the book, it can summed up in three simple words: **THOUGHTS BECOME THINGS.**

I actually don't' like that they relegate the conceptual idea of the Law of Attraction into these three words, because it oversimplifies its truth.

And besides that, even according to the Law of Attraction, our thoughts don't actually become our things. Our **BELIEFS** become our things.

A thought can be flippant and fleeting. It can change with the winds. But our belief system... our deepest, truest, most honest personal beliefs that lie within all of us... **THAT** is what is playing in all of our lives. What have we allowed ourselves to be conditioned to believe in?

WHY DOES CONDITIONING WORK? Because we have faith in our beliefs. **WE HAVE FAITH IN WHAT WE BELIEVE IN.** Remember what my friend Kris Prochaska said? We are constantly searching for evidence all around us to prove that we are right.

The power and energy you exude from a single, solitary, relentless, undeniable belief in something is enormous. The energy from that moment is magnetic, quite literally.

When you know that you're standing on the precipice of something great... it's no surprise that within a short time period you find yourself experiencing something you knew beyond a shadow of a doubt you would experience. You attracted that experience to you by your undeniable belief in the truth of its existence.

THE ELEMENT OF FAITH

Most world spiritual leaders would tell you that **FAITH** is what changes everything. Faith is defined as *"the complete trust or confidence in someone else or something."*

The problem with the word "faith" is that most people mistake it for the word "hope," not with their vocabulary, but with their actions. And then they treat the word "hope" like it's a "wish," and they make wishes all throughout life, as if they were blowing out the candles on a giant birthday cake... hoping that maybe – just maybe... some giant fairy in the sky will answer if they're good enough.

And when the fairies don't come, and the choirs don't sing, and life falls down all around you, you look back on your dreams and think none of it worked, and you say, *"I had faith..."* but you never actually did. You just had a little sprinkle of hope that you wished upon yourself.

FAITH can and should be broken down into a more aptly usable, reliable, and consistent word called **CONFIDENCE.**

The millionaires Hill interviewed also all had another common denominator, outside of knowing exactly what they wanted. They all believed, without question, that they could have what they were working for.

There were no *"self-worth"* issues on the table, or constant *"self-doubt,"* or *"personal reflection"* that led to *"self-loathing"* and wondering if *"you're truly capable or worthy of whatever it is you're working for."*

THEY ALL HAD CONFIDENCE.

When was the last time you did something with relentless confidence? You just *"knew"* that it would all eventually work out. You're not sure how, or why, or when, or where...but the *"IF"* was answered from the beginning. Confidence is removing the *"if's"* from our vernacular. Confidence in whatever it is that we're doing changes everything. The energy of confidence attracts like energy.

John Paul DeJoria went door-to-door, selling Christmas cards and newspapers to help support his family at the age of 10. He was eventually sent to live in the foster care system in Los Angeles, joined a gang, and was otherwise living without shit, help, or hope. And then he decided to join the military, got out, borrowed $700 from someone to create a new company, slept in his car while going door-to-door (again) trying to sell his new shampoo.... And to date, Paul Mitchell Systems revenues over 1 billion dollars a year.

You know what he said when being interviewed once about how he was able to stay faithful to his dream, even when living in his car, selling door-to-door?

HE NEVER STOPPED FEELING CONFIDENT IN WHAT HE WAS BUILDING.

THE ART OF THE BULLSHIT

BUT THIS IS THE MILLION DOLLAR QUESTION:

HOW DO YOU HAVE CONFIDENCE WHEN YOU'RE STANDING IN THE MIDDLE OF A SHIT LIFE?

How do you have confidence when your life has been one long series of disappointments, failures, let down's, and fuck ups, one right after the next...as if they were all just waiting their turn in line to kick you in the ass?

How do you have confidence when there is no evidence that you can or should? And the secret answer to this goes beyond the Law of Attraction or a Napoleon Hill research book.

This is what I've discovered.

HOW DO YOU PERSONALLY CREATE SOMETHING FROM NOTHING?

The recipe for this level of success is what separates us from the other mammals on earth. It's the one single "*human*" ability that elevates us beyond instinct. And it is the ability to consistently think and act, independent of any situation we are in, and stay confident in and confidently focused on what is ahead.

The greatest lion in the greatest jungle still acts on instincts only. The smallest child in the biggest world, however, can learn to think independent of their situation. This is the beauty of a cognitive reasoning rationale.

Being able to stand in the middle of nothing and believe in something is an art form. And it takes more than a modicum of strength that very few people on this planet have.

I believe it's the art of thinking independent of what's happening around you. It's the art what seems like *"bullshitting"* yourself momentarily to believe in something greater. Some people call it bullshitting. Fake it until you make it. Dress the part before you get it. It's all the same.

It's about changing our internal belief system. It's about focusing on something outside of the shit storm you're standing in the middle of. It's about being able to **ACT INDEPENDENT OF WHAT IS HAPPENING AROUND YOU and MOVE CONFIDENTALLY IN THE DIRECTION OF YOUR DREAMS.**

When was the last time you were capable of acting and living outside of your own reality, and acting independently of what you see around you... going for something greater than you've seen, bigger than you know?

Most people are only willing to flirt with confidence and not actually marry it. You're willing to talk about it, take it to dinner, even invest in it a bit... but give up everything for it, sleep in your car for it, leave your husband for it, quit your job for it... no chance.

So be honest with yourself again here. You're not living some epic life because you've been too chicken shit to really have confidence in what exists ahead of you. You are living in the reality of what's behind you to have confidence in more.

The job failed. The people disappointed. He left. She cheated. It all went to shit. Everyone sucks. No one is real. Nothing works out. And this is where you live.

BUT you can stand up in the middle of this shit and say, "*EVEN THOUGH THIS IS WHERE I LIVE PHYSICALLY I am going to start today moving out of here mentally, emotionally, and spiritually.*"

WRITE THIS ON YOUR MIRROR: I AM GREATER THAN THE LION. You are greater than the most powerful king of the jungle because...

YOU have the ability to look around you and **BE** different, **THINK** different, ACT different... and physically, mentally and emotionally **WALK AWAY.**

George Soros, one of the richest people in the world, survived the Nazi occupation of Hungary after his dad paid someone to let him pretend to be his godson. In 1947, he escaped the country, fled to London, eventually put himself through school, and from absolutely nothing, created what he is today.

Not only was he born without that silver spoon in his mouth, he was also born into extreme poverty and a life threatening situation. Yet somehow he found the will to build something new, to create someone he wasn't before, to become something he had never known.

PART. 9

THE SUBJUGATION OF MY HUMAN EXISTENCE

YOU ARE A SPIRITUAL BEING HAVING A HUMAN EXPERIENCE.

It is imperative that you discover how to find your way back to the Source from which you came. It is essential for your continued growth that you plug back into your Higher Source.

You are on the precipice of illuminating a single truth within you: that you are a spiritual giant who is awakening from a slumber to slay the dragons of your world. YOU ARE THE HERO.

YOU ARE THE WARRIOR THE WORLD HAS BEEN WAITING FOR.
THE (ALMOST) AFTERLIFE OF KRISTY SINSARA

Have you ever had a supernatural experience in your life? And by *supernatural* I mean an experience that involved anything outside of the "human" realm of this world. I have had several. I used to feel like I could feel angels around me when I was a kid. In fact, they seemed so real that I used to talk to them sometimes when I was a child. I still do actually.

There are some "*spiritual*" or "*super natural*" experiences that some of us just can't explain; and the truth is so real that no one could ever take the experience from us.

HERE IS ONE OF MY "NEAR DEATH" EXPERIENCES...

I was about 32 years old, and I had just bought a new Acura LS. The car was about 2 years old, drove like a dream, never had an issue. If you've ever had the pleasure of owning a relatively new Acura you're aware that these cars are quite "*dreamy*" on the road. They run like they're gliding, and they very infrequently have problems.

And I only explain all of this to you to "*out*" reason and argue the natural logical part of your brain that will instantly search for rationale and logic to explain the "*unexplainable*" story I'm about to tell you. Sometimes you just can't explain certain things. This car never had this (or any) issue before or after this moment. So for me, this incident gets chalked up to one of the craziest, super-natural, near-death experiences of this human existence.

One morning I was sitting at a four-way intersection. I was the first car in line waiting for the light to turn green. It was 2-lane traffic on all sides around me. I noticed a strange phenomenon: Everyone was pulling up behind me (and I'm not in a left turn lane), so there's literally no reason for this at all. No one has come up beside me. There are literally probably ten cars stacked behind my car. "*Strange*," I think, as I instantly dismiss what's happening. The speed limit going both directions was 60mph. As the light turned green, I immediately pounded my accelerator pedal, as I always do, to move forward. However, this time the pedal went all the way down the floorboard of the car, and the car didn't move.

"*What the hell?*" I thought. This had never happened before. What in the hell is going on? I instantly started pounding the accelerator again and again, nothing.

And then, all of a sudden, like a freight train rushing towards me out of thin air, a huge semi-truck ran the red light going perpendicular to me, going roughly 70mph. As it was rushing through the intersection it began to vigorously honk the horn, fast and furiously warning the upcoming traffic; as if the driver is letting everyone know that it cannot stop for some reason.

And the instant realization rushes through my veins, "*HAD MY ACCELERATOR JUST WORKED IN THIS MOMENT THIS HUGE TRUCK WOULD HAVE JUST T-BONED MY DOOR.*" Who knows what would have happened? However, I know what could have happened. I could have died. I could have been instantly paralyzed. I could have been disfigured. A number of things were possible; and certainly life has shown us that people have had all of the above experiences with less than a semi-truck T-boning them at 70mph. The consequences could have been grave.

But they weren't. There weren't any consequences, because in this highly improbable, seemingly impossible moment my accelerator stopped working... as if to say, "*I've got this one, trust me.*"

I was so shaken up by the realization of what had just happened, I just sat there in my car, until the cars behind me started honking. And... of course, the minute I went to hit my accelerator again, the car drove like a dream, as it always had before.

As I slowly start driving off, the car behind pulled up beside me and a man motioned for me to roll down my window. I rolled it down, and he said, "*That was insane. Had you actually gone when that light turned green you and I both would probably be dead right now.*" I didn't have time to explain to him that I tried to go... but my car wouldn't let me.

Yes... that was insane!

I BELIEVE...IN SOMETHING MORE REALISTIC THAN SANTA

I am believer in Theistic Evolution, Creationism Evolution. This means that I believe that God (a higher power, energy, or Source) orchestrated all of Evolution.

I believe this because I cannot fathom the concept that the finite, intricate necessities that make all of life come together just happen to be by "*chance*." However, I also don't believe in the idea that some great God in the sky created two people who fucked up in the first millisecond of humanity and decided to punish the rest of us for it for eternity.

Both seem so ridiculously and childishly insane that I lean on a level of science and faith coming together to process things mindfully and cognitively that my brain cannot otherwise understand.

For me there is a level of science and faith that must come together to even begin to appropriately process a near-death experience. For me the process starts outside of myself. The reality that I'm certainly not the only person who has had an experience that was directed by some super natural phenomenon which led to saving a life.

Look at Lynn Jennifer Groesbeck's experience. When she was 25 years old she lost control of her car and landed in the icy Spanish Fork River in Utah. Fourteen hours later first responders found her 18-month old daughter hanging upside down, just slightly above the freezing river waters. The responders stated that just a few hours before this they heard an adult woman's voice yell "*Help me*" from inside the car. Yet they discovered that the voice could not have come from the young woman, as it was later discovered that she had died upon impact. No one can explain the voice they heard, or how an infant could survive hanging upside down for 14 hours in freezing temperatures.

Or how about the story of Donnie Register, who was working as a cashier at a local convenient store. One night two men came to rob him. As they pulled a gun out and fired directly at him, he put his hands up in self-defense. The bullet hit his wedding ring and was deflected. He had pieces of the bullet lodged in his throat, but nothing was life threatening and he was fine.

And these are just two of literally thousands upon thousands of countless experiences of others all over this globe, all throughout history.

People died and came back to life. Someone was saved by someone else having a strange and unexplainable "*feeling*" to find them. Hikers being led to safety by a strange voice in the woods guiding them. Voices across radio transmitters which led to finding someone in trouble, only to discover there was no radio transmission available.

My beautiful friend, Julia Junkin, who is also a Sufi Healer and great spiritual guide, once told me that the more tapped into the spirit world I become, the more it will reveal itself to me.

I believe this to be true. It is congruent with my experience that the more I am willing to open my mind to possibilities I do not understand, and experiences I cannot explain, and ideas that I will never fully be able to conceive, the more all of the above will show itself to me.

THAT WHICH HITS YOU COULD NEVER HAVE MISSED YOU

It's like what Billy Fingers taught us, where he reminds us after death that there are certain crossroads we all reach in life. Crossroads we were destined to reach. And it doesn't matter which road we take, which page we turn to, which person we marry, which job we take – because in the end, we wind up in certain places, irrespective of those personal choices made.

Remember (again), as the Sufi's say, "*That which hits you could never have missed you.*" Meaning: the big things in life that hit you, that change you and alter your way of being, thinking, or living, could never have missed you. Meaning: you didn't orchestrate all of the things that, in the end, made the most sense.

This is one of the most powerful realities of your life because if you can truly understand that you're only seeing what you want to see then you can learn to train your mind, your heart, and (more importantly), your energy, to **SEE MORE OF WHAT YOU WANT TO SEE IN YOUR LIFE.**

I tell this story with gratitude, but I also say it with great trepidation because I believe that one of the most horrifically self-centered statements someone can make is, "*Thank God that I was saved.*"

To allude to the fact that God chose you, out of all others, to save; as if your life is somehow suddenly more important that all of the others who died that day.

So how do you explain a *"super-natural, near-death"* experience to someone who doesn't believe in the egocentric destiny of one's life?

That's the greatest thing about it all. We see what we want to see. And perhaps a near-death experience is to help push those of us who need to see something a little more tangible and personal to tether our hearts to the truth of all possibilities around us.

Had it not been for my own experiences, I wouldn't be so certain that near-death experiences are plausible. Yet here I am, telling you that you couldn't possibly take my experience from me, as it's already changed me from the inside out.

It molded a portion of my mind that now says, *"I don't need to explain the unexplainable, and I can truly just allow faith to be what it was originally supposed to be for me: complete confidence in the unknown."*

Was this the purpose?
For me, the answer is yes.

HOW I FOUND MY WAY BACK TO GOD...

So let's start with some truths, which even the hardest of hearts can't deny...

There is one single consistency throughout all of humanity, from the cavemen to the current man... written on the walls throughout time, in all of civilizations, memorialized in history from Egypt to Alaska, from the natives to the nomads...

And it is NOT our collective need in humanity to understand each other, or love, or to find success, or find alien life forms on other planets. The single consistency throughout all of humanity is our collective desire to **FIND GOD.**

There are many unanswered questions in life...things we may never know, answers that can't be understood in this life... but I find it interesting, inspiring actually, that regardless of our age, sex, religious ideologies or life experiences, we all have this one desire at the core of us... and that desire is to constantly plug back into the source from which we came.

Believe me when I say... **YOU ARE A SPIRITUAL BEING HAVING A HUMAN EXPERIENCE...** and the more you deviate in your life from this truth, the more you will feel out of alignment.

Stay focused on the things that truly matter in life, and the things that truly matter will focus on you.

Now, let me tell you how I came to this conclusion, and the powerful reality behind this truth for you.

I grew up in an abusive religious environment. What is an "*abusive religious environment*," you ask? There are many forms actually, but for me it's where there is an extreme discrepancy between what you're being told is "*truth*" and what you're seeing being played out in your daily life. Religious abuse also looks like "*shoving religious ideologies down your throat*" and forcing you (literally) to acquiesce to someone else's belief system.

The truth is that religion is someone else's interpretation of God; spirituality is your own discovery and interpretation and understanding.

By the very nature of a religion itself, you are capitulating to believing in how someone experienced God for themselves. And I believe that we are moving more and more into a spiritual age. I truly believe that the Universe (Or God... same thing to me) has called forth a masterful bounty of individuals who are plugged into "*Source*" and are using their lives to bring a new collective awareness to this planet, a new collective consciousness. And the beautiful thing is that this new particular wave of understanding isn't specifically tethered to a interpretation.

I can tell you my beliefs or interpretations of life, or how I have come to believe in God, and you can take it or leave it. It's "*my*" truth, not necessarily yours. Or we can share our ideas together and come to a conclusion that we may agree upon. The beauty of free thinking is that there is no narrative that must be followed, outside of the fact that there is no narrative that must be followed.

So, fear not, you're not going to hell if you don't agree with this chapter.

I STOLE JESUS FROM THE CHURCH

The truth is that I truly cannot recall a single moment of my childhood where anyone emulated the character of Jesus Christ. Church was literally just a social event. We may as well have been going to the Kentucky Derby every Sunday for that matter.

I certainly don't look back on my childhood and remember anyone single person who I thought really personified the concept of *"Christianity,"*

However, it wasn't these realities that drew me away from God; it was my parents. It was watching my dad attempt to sexually abuse me Monday through Saturday and then sit in a choir pew singing church hymns with his eyes closed, shaking everyone's hands and hugging and smiling and laughing.

It is actually a mind-blowing, totally unfathomable, dumbfounding reality for me to consider that my parents ever thought they were raising us as *"Christians."*

I look back now and question why they thought this. Because we carried Bibles and got dressed up and went to church 100 days a year?

I came into this world spiritually enlightened enough to understand that what I witnessed at church was not God. And you didn't even need to have a spiritual bone in your body to realize that what I was witnessing at home certainly wasn't God.

It was a man on display, pretending to be there for God.

The truth is that I was so turned off by my childhood experiences of this constant hypocrisy in my face that I eventually turned away from it all, completely.

When I left home, I left it all behind me.
God's not real. Church is dumb. My parents are liars.
Well... two out of three turned out to be true.

And I stayed in a state of trying my hardest to scrape off any of the last of the religion off of me, out of me, away from me. It was all just gross and yucky.

I never prayed. I never sought. I never read. I never wondered. I was happy to just be away from the crazy, from the hypocrisy, and from the abuse of it all.

GOD ISN'T ACTUALLY AS SMALL AND ORDINARY (or as white) AS THE CHURCH PRETENDS.

Until one day, randomly, while in my early 20's and living out in California, a friend invited me to a church called "*Agape International Center for Truth.*"

I was intrigued enough to go. The truth is that although I needed to wash away past experiences of my childhood, I was longing for a connection I was missing, and I wasn't sure how or why... so when my friend invited me, I gratefully accepted her invitation.

I drove to this church the next day and walked into a Sunday service. I was instantly captivated by the energy in the room. I was mesmerized by the diversity in the room as well.

I sat down in a chair, and a Jewish Rabbi came to sit next to me; a few minutes later, a Catholic Priest to the left of me. A Muslim in front of me. Buddhists all around me.

This was it. **THIS** experience. **THIS** was God. This was life. This was US. This was the power source I instantly felt drawn to, and it was the recognizable power source that I knew was familiar to my core.

The first service I was there, Arun Ghandi spoke (Mahatma Ghandi's grandson). He spoke to us of the importance of sharing our joy, our pain, our sorrow, and our laughter together within our families.

He shared with us a story about how he was sick once and could only eat soup, so everyone in his family only consumed soup with him while he was sick until he was feeling better. He shared the importance of why everyone should do this.

I was literally taken aback. I was completely captivated by this entire experience. **THIS IS IT. THIS IS GOD.**

It was nothing like the experiences I grew up with where people were singing songs repetitively, in a slight crescendo, to create an evocative experience from an otherwise totally ordinary moment.

You didn't need music to feel God there. God is everywhere. There was no need to manipulate a presence that was otherwise not known, or felt, or seen. I could feel the energy surging through my being, again. It was a feeling that was strangely familiar, yet I knew that I had never experienced anything like this growing up in Oklahoma.

I consistently went back to that church, over and over. I soaked up this energy, and I let those moments feed my soul.

Michael Beckwith was the minister of this community. I had no idea who he was at the time, and I would later come to appreciate that it was him who brought me back to this existence and truth that I always knew was there. So when he participated in creating "*The Secret,*" I was all too familiar with his teachings and practices.

The next Sunday as I was visiting, the speaker was Les Brown. Unbelievable. He is one of the most powerfully-inspiring, life-motivating speakers I have ever known. I was again enthralled by his words. Moved to action by his passion.

I found myself leaning on the edge of my chair as he was speaking, longing for the passion within him to find its way to me.

Every single one of my experiences with this spiritual community was empowering, enlightening, inspiring, and motivating; but above all things for me... they were all honest and true.

I stayed in alignment with this energy, and I stayed connected to this spiritual power source, for the duration of my time in California.

I look back on my early 20's and the fact that the church I grew up in caused me to question whether or not I believed in a God at all, and I feel so grateful that this friend – who I strangely never saw again after she asked me if I wanted to go – had unknowingly opened this portal for me and introduced me back into a space my soul was longing for. This was the first introduction to truth.

However, my spirit desperately longed for more answers as they related to God. I decided to study theology in college. Yes, I was **THAT** interested in discovering truths.

After I eventually made my way back home to Oklahoma, I enrolled in Mid-America Bible College where I became a student of theology.

I was truly captivated by my studies. I was enthralled in this vortex of truth and knowledge. I was so interested in learning more about the Bible and theology that I actually took a 7:30 am class, and was never late.

If you knew me personally, you would know that this was simply significant proof of my love for what I was learning.

Finally, I got to take Theology 1. I was sitting in class 20 minutes earlier than needed. The professor walked in (and remember, this is a Christian University I am attending), and he said:

"Good morning, class. Welcome to Theology 1. I give this disclaimer at the beginning of all semesters for this class. If any of you are wavering in your faith at all, and you feel it's important to remain a Christian, I would strongly encourage you to get up, walk out now. For the rest of you, I can almost assure you that by the end of this semester, you will all become Atheists."

I thought: **HOLY SHIT**. This is going to be so amazing!!! One guy in the back got up and walked out.

And the class began.

I was so captivated from second one that I felt like I'd lost my mind in some hypnotic intellectual orgasm.

I had no idea why, but I was the most fascinated with the study of religion. I have always been immensely enchanted with the truth, as it relates to God.

I go on in my studies to take Greek, Hebrew, Ancient Aramaic Languages, the lost languages of the Bible, Theology II, The Books of the New Testament, World Religions and Popular Cults, The Life of Paul, the Lost Books of the Bible, The Book of Thomas, The Dead Sea Scrolls, The Septuagint, and on and on.

And I was just as fascinated with each of these classes as I was on that first day of Theology.

I decided that I was going to go on to Philips University Seminary after this and get my doctorate in Theological Studies.

Suddenly, all I wanted to do was learn and absorb truth. That was the truth I had always been seeking.

Truth that was not manipulated by an agenda or held to a limitation of someone's understanding; but an actual truth that exists whether we are capable of forming a coherent single thought around it or not.

A TRUTH LIKE GRAVITY.

A truth that doesn't need you to believe in it or understand how it works in order for it TO work.

A truth that exists independent of our comprehension of its composition and origin.

And the realization that I could go jump off a tall building and scream all of the way down that I don't believe in gravity, but gravity doesn't care. Because it's a truth that cannot be altered in any capacity by our human existence, knowledge, or understanding.

THESE are the truths that I seek.

A TRUTH LIKE THE LAW OF ATTRACTION.

The reality that all that I believe in is manifesting before me. It's not a mystical truth that needs you to subscribe to some specific religion in order for it to work.

My mother believes in the law of attraction and uses the power of it constantly. She calls it faith in Jesus. But her faith in Jesus is actually so strong that she can manifest through this faith whatever it is that she's believing for.

Let me share with you one of her "*faith*" experiences. She wanted to sell her car once, many years ago. She wrote in an envelope the amount she'd like to sell it for and the date she'd like to sell it by. Then she prayed and asked, and then offered gratitude, for the sale. She tucked the envelope in her drawer and went on with her life.

Six months later a man knocked on her door and asked if there's any chance she'd like to sell the car outside of her home (which did not, by the way, have a For Sale sign on it), because it's the exact car that his daughter is looking for. And yes, of course, he also offered her the exact amount she had written down.

Coincidence? That's about as coincidental as my accelerator pedal not working the very second a semi-truck is running a red light to T-bone me.

If I can convey one single thing to all of my Oklahoma friends who grew up in church (and others like them), as I did, and who have been longing for something more than the man-made sounds of a clanking tambourine singing a repetitive verse to manipulate your emotions and provoke a feeling that something is happening within you (outside of your serotonin levels rising from the excitement around you)... DO ME A FAVOR.

Trust me, right now, in this moment. Believe in the truth that you know exists within you. THERE IS MORE THAN YOU'VE EVER BEEN TAUGHT.

God cannot be relegated to a specific religion or concept. God is not in need of your praise and your forgiveness.

God is not longing for you to suppress your quests for truth. You are longing for more than the God of your childhood; and you long for more, because there is MORE to receive.

All that we seek is seeking us, my friends. All of our desires in this life are on the other side of the mountain. You must conquer your doubts and your fears, and the riches of the kingdom will await you.

GOD IS MOVING THROUGH YOU, AS YOU.

Jesus Christ said, in the book of Thomas: The Kingdom of God is inside of you, and all around you. Not in a mansion of wood and stone. Split a piece of wood, and I am there. Lift a stone and you will find me.

Jesus Christ was right. And he was very real. And his words have been manipulated and stolen for an agenda of which he did not agree to.

I urge you to not turn your backs on God because the church you experienced didn't represent the hope within you that God is real. God is real, as you are real.

But it is incumbent upon you to discover this truth for yourself. This is one way that you must be like Jesus. He was a truth seeker. As you are, as am I.

Your salvation does not lie in the words or understandings of anyone before you, it lies within you. It lies as you, all around you. All you must do is ask to be shown the truth, and the truth will show you what you seek.

There is no mystical need for priests, and fires, and dragons and Books. There is only a need to go within, and quiet your mind, and listen to the whisper calling to you.

YOU ARE HERE FOR GREATNESS.
YOU WERE MADE FOR GREATNESS.

And I swear to you that you alone hold the power to unlock the riches of heaven. FIND YOUR STRENGTH.

AND CHOOSE TO ALWAYS REMAIN DIVINELY INSPIRED.

A GUIDED MEDITATION THAT WILL HELP EMPOWER YOU THROUGH HEALING AND CHANGE

One of my personal spiritual practices is to meditate, as often as I can. One of my favorite things to do is to create guided meditations for those who have been where I used to be and help usher them into a new awareness using this daily practice.

I'd like to invite you to practice this meditation with me.

I want you to imagine that you can see an older (future) version of yourself sitting on top of a mountain. This version of yourself has already done all of the work you are doing now. They've become enlightened on epic levels, they understand truth without judgment, they have worked through all of the pain inside of you, and they exist only in a space of wholeness, illuminating your light for others to see.

They are a spiritual giant, and wildly in touch with this reality. They are the version of yourself that (in your wildest dreams) you have always wanted to become.

Imagine them sitting on the mountaintop, underneath a sea of stars. They're meditating. You can feel the energy radiating from them. And I want you to imagine that you're walking up the mountain towards them.

You can sense that they're aware of your presence but are not moved by it. They remain still, and focused. You realize they are channeling the energy of the Universe all around them, into them.

You slowly continue to walk towards them, taking in the experience of seeing this magnificent being before you, feeling almost overwhelmed by the truth that this is you.

Eventually you are in the same space, and you are face to face with your older self. You are taken aback by their beauty, their wholeness of energy, and their power.

BUILD SOME QUIET TIME AND ASK...AND LISTEN...

You begin a conversation:

"I need your help. I need you to show me how we did this. How did we become this thing that you are? How did we get to this place of ultimate peace, and joy, and acceptance, and enlightenment?

I am asking you to guide me. Be my truth. Be my eyes. I need you to illuminate all that is wrong and all that is right with my life so that I may be able to clearly see the direction before me and the choices ahead of me. How do I become you? Please show me."

And then your future self turns to you and says, "And so it shall be for you. You are about to embark upon a great journey. And I will be beside you the whole way...until eventually someday...we merge into one."

Open your eyes...and say *"Thank you."*

THE EPIC CONCLUSION... IS THIS...

Writing this book has been the single most healing thing I have ever done in my life. It has created self-awareness within me, and a purpose beyond me, that I can now see past anything I have ever known. I'm not sure how it all ends for me, but I know the new beginning before me.

As you begin on your own journey I want you to imagine that we are going to take this walk together. I am here with you, every single step along the way. I am holding your hand, if need be. I can walk beside you, or gently behind you, reassuring you of each step that you take. I want you to know that you are not alone.

There is nothing more important in your life than your ability to see this through, as I have. I cannot convey to you, in mere human words, the chorus within me that is now being sung. I am finally standing in the light of freedom, showered with the beauty of the truth that lies within me: I can truly do all things through the Christ within that strengthens me. It is an epic prelude to a wonderful journey ahead.

Welcome to this journey, my fellow wanderer. Your path awaits you...

> **NOT ALL WHO WANDER ARE LOST.**
> Endings are also new beginnings... it's all a matter of perspective.

WHERE'S THE EVIDENCE? I'll leave you with one last, final thought, which is to remember to always show evidence (daily) of what you truly want, and what you truly believe in life. For instance, you're not allowed to say you really want a new life but do absolutely nothing towards changing anything about your current life. There's no evidence to support what you say. Your actions **MUST** match your words. **PROOF** of your desires will show up in your actions. So make a promise to yourself to commit to showing yourself that you really are ready for something more (in every aspect of your life), and then get ready to **BE** something more, so that you can **HAVE** something more!

I love you.

Sincerely, Sinsara

Kristy Sinsara

FOREWORD
(BUT REALLY THE BACKWARD)

BY REVEREND JANE HIATT

"*It's not my fault!*" I protested to my mom when I was 9. She'd pointed out the ice cream dribbled all over my t-shirt. I really meant: "*I didn't do it on purpose.*" This book is about taking responsibility even for things we didn't do "*on purpose.*" Our actions stem from beliefs stored in our subconscious and so often seem out of our control. Because we didn't consciously plan an action, we don't get why we keep getting into situations and it seems like we shouldn't be held accountable. It seems unfair. But we must seize responsibility. It is a super power.

As the responsible party for our own lives, we stop arguing about whose fault an experience is and start wondering what hidden beliefs are in play. Just wondering can be transforming because it puts our subconscious and our higher power on notice that we are ready for change and want some answers! The tools Kristy offers will get us started exposing those mistaken beliefs so we can start changing them.

What I love most about Kristy Sinsara's work is her courage and transparency with her life stories. Instead of hiding in the shadows of shame or making excuses for her choices, she used my mother's logic: any "ice cream on the shirt" is the doing of the one wearing the shirt. In sharing these stories, she inspires all of us to look more closely at the places we are stuck and the excuses we are making for being stuck. Because Kristy took 100% responsibility, she found freedom and a much greater self-acceptance and self-love and she paved the way for the rest of us to do the same.

I feel so honored to have witnessed Kristy's subconscious explorations. I watched her hesitantly befriend her 3-year old self, knowing the challenges the child held for her. I felt the shift when Kristy made a powerful intention to play bigger. Free People World and the book in your hands are her first steps in fulfilling that promise. And I sensed the light in the room as she connected with her guides and angels for the first time. I have watched her transform into a more soulful and true version of herself.

But this book is not about Kristy — even though it is full of her stories. This book is about what is possible for each of us. What is possible for you. Never tell yourself that Kristy is special, a crazy Ninja who can do anything. She is and she can. But so can you. You too can face your shadow, find your inner child, and access your spiritual power.

Kristy is passionate to make a difference in the world, to ease the suffering of people who have shared the same challenges and hurts that she endured. Pain is never the final chapter. There is so much more that we can be and experience if we will just take ownership of our lives.

If you wonder if what she promises could really apply to you, stop wondering. Believe. Trade your excuses for power. Show up fully. An epic life is just waiting for you to claim it.

- Rev. Jane Hiatt

Find me on Facebook at **www.facebook.com/ksinsara**
Follow my blogs at **www.kristysinsara.org**

Write to me at:
Kristy Sinsara
2689 NW Crossing Drive
Bend, Oregon 97703

If you are interested in joining me, and other life-coaches, on a life-changing, world-destination, self-help retreat, please visit

www.freepeopleworld.com

There is no greater way to kick start the new you!

OTHER BOOKS BY THIS AUTHOR:

PERSONAL DEVELOPMENT
Forty Life Lessons
The Top Ten Rules to Marriage
The Daily Ninja – 60-Day Journal

BUSINESS DEVELOPMENT
How to Become a Social Media Strategist
How to Build Your Business Using Social Media

Made in the USA
San Bernardino, CA
09 February 2018